Foundations of Contemporary Interpretation
Moisés Silva, Series Editor
Volume 3

LITERARY APPROACHES TO BIBLICAL INTERPRETATION

Tremper Longman III

Academie Books Grand Rapids, Michigan
Zondervan Publishing House

Literary Approaches to Biblical Interpretation
Copyright © 1987 by Tremper Longman III

ACADEMIE BOOKS is an imprint of Zondervan Publishing House
1415 Lake Drive, S.E.,
Grand Rapids, Michigan 49506

Library of Congress Cataloging in Publication Data

Longman, Tremper.
    Literary approaches to biblical interpretation.

    (Foundations of contemporary interpretation; v. 3)
    Bibliography: p.
    Includes index.
    1. Bible as literature.   I. Title.   II. Series: Foundations of
contemporary interpretation; v. 3.
BS535.L58   1987   220.6'6   87–14567
ISBN 0–310–40941–1

Edited by Craig Noll
Designed by Louise Bauer

Printed in the United States of America

87   88   89   90   91   92 / CH / 10   9   8   7   6   5   4   3   2   1

To my wife, Alice,
and our three children,
Tremper IV, Timothy, and Andrew

CONTENTS

EDITOR'S PREFACE

Among the various academic disciplines, literary criticism would appear to have the greatest potential for shedding light on the task of biblical hermeneutics. For a variety of reasons, however, biblical scholarship has until recently paid little attention to this field. In particular, conservative exegetes have, not without reason, feared that the use of literary criticism leads to a downplaying or even the denial of the historical worth of Scripture.

It is all the more gratifying, therefore, that, for the present series, we have been able to secure the services of a young scholar whose work blends an intelligent commitment to the authority of the Bible with an impressive expertise in contemporary literary theories. Professor Longman's doctoral research into a specialized area of Akkadian literature led him to examine in considerable detail competing approaches to literary criticism. He has since continued to pursue an interdisciplinary approach to biblical exegesis. For example, with a view to gaining a deeper understanding of the field, he participated, under a 1984 grant from the National Endowment for the Humanities, in a semiotics seminar at Princeton University directed by the eminent scholar Michael Shapiro.

The author has nurtured a special interest in biblical poetry, as reflected in a 1982 article in *Biblica* on the thorny question of Hebrew meter, a more popular work entitled *How to Read the Psalms,* and several other projects. Clearly, Professor Longman's work is not merely theoretical, and his commitment to wrestle with the details of the biblical text shows through in the present volume.

I am delighted to be able to introduce volume 3 of

Foundations of Contemporary Interpretation as a substantive and significant contribution to the task of biblical hermeneutics. Readers with little prior knowledge of modern literary theories will appreciate the clarity with which the field is described in this book. Students of literature, on the other hand, will be particularly grateful for a work that identifies, with commendable balance, the points of contact between literary criticism and biblical interpretation. Without ignoring the difficult questions, Professor Longman has pointed the way for a responsible "reading strategy" in Bible study.

Moisés Silva

ACKNOWLEDGMENTS

My interest in the interaction between literary studies and ancient literature began during graduate work at Yale University. My dissertation focused on a particular literary genre in Akkadian, and I had occasion to examine contemporary theory to see what literary scholars were saying on the subject. In this effort I received much good guidance from my adviser W. W. Hallo. This initial contact with literary studies led me to continue my studies in the intersection between literary theory and ancient literature.

I soon came in contact with the vast secondary literature on the subject of literary approaches to the study of the Bible. As I discovered, there was both much of value and also much to discard in this literature. I trust that the present volume will aid the student and scholar in getting a foothold in this subdiscipline and will answer questions for ministers and laypeople who may have wanted more information about the literary approach to the Bible.

I thank my colleague Moisés Silva for guidance and criticism during the writing of this book. I am grateful also to other associates at Westminster Theological Seminary and elsewhere for their thoughtful advice and assistance on the manuscript: Raymond Dillard, Vern Poythress, Bruce Waltke, Alan Groves, Samuel Logan, Douglas Green, Steven McKenzie, V. Phillips Long, and Richard Whitekettle.

Unless noted otherwise, I use the New International Version in Scripture quotations. In poetic analyses, however, I have rearranged some of the poetic structure. I frequently depart from the NIV in chapter 7. Chapter 2 was presented in an earlier form as a lecture to the Institute of Biblical Research and then published as "The Literary Approach to the Study of the Old Testament: Promise and Pitfalls" in *JETS* 28 (1985): 385–98. It is used by permission of the editor.

My final thanks go to my wife and three sons, who are a source of love and encouragement to me.

ABBREVIATIONS

Bib	*Biblica*
BJRL	*Bulletin of the John Rylands Library*
CBQ	*Catholic Biblical Quarterly*
EI	*Eretz Israel*
FOTL	*Forms of the Old Testament Literature, Eerdmans*
HTR	*Harvard Theological Review*
IDB	*The Interpreter's Dictionary of the Bible*
JBL	*Journal of Biblical Literature*
JETS	*Journal of the Evangelical Theological Society*
JQRS	*Jewish Quarterly Review Supplement*
JSNT	*Journal for the Study of the New Testament*
JSOT	*Journal for the Study of the Old Testament*
NTS	*New Testament Studies*
SJT	*Scottish Journal of Theology*
VT	*Vetus Testamentum*
WTJ	*Westminster Theological Journal*
ZAW	*Zeitschrift für die alttestamentliche Wissenschaft*

INTRODUCTION

A weekend seminar on marriage takes place at a local church. A well-known Christian counselor has flown in to instruct the young couples about relationships. During the afternoon session on sexuality, the counselor begins by reading Song of Songs 1:2–4:

> Let him kiss me with the kisses of his mouth—
> for your love is more delightful than wine.
> Pleasing is the fragrance of your perfumes;
> your name is like perfume poured out.
> No wonder the maidens love you!
> Take me away with you—let us hurry!
> The king has brought me into his chambers.

Most modern students of the Bible would feel few qualms about applying this Scripture passage to human sexual relationships. A century ago, however, such an application of the Song of Songs would have aroused much uneasiness, and five hundred years ago a preacher might be dismissed from the church or worse if he taught that the book was a collection of poems about human love rather than an allegory of the relationship between Christ and the church.

A reflective reader of the Psalms begins Psalm 2:

> Why do the nations rage
> and the peoples plot in vain?

1

> The kings of the earth take their stand
>   and the rulers gather together
> against the Lord
>   and against his Anointed One.
> "Let us break their chains," they say,
>   "and throw off their fetters."

While studying this passage, the reader observes much repetition between the lines. How should such repetition be taken? Are the parallel lines saying the same thing, using different words? Are they perhaps not really repeating at all? Are there both repetition and progression in the lines?

Finally, the following verses strike quite a different tone:

> And I saw a beast coming out of the sea. He had ten horns and seven heads, with ten crowns on his horns, and on each head a blasphemous name. The beast I saw resembled a leopard, but had feet like those of a bear and a mouth like a that of a lion. (Rev. 13:1–2)

How should this passage be interpreted? Is it a *literal* description of a future event? Or is it *figurative*?

Such questions, at least in part, are *literary* questions and are of major importance to the correct interpretation of Scripture. The reading from the Song of Songs raises the question of genre identification (see chapter 4). Psalm 2 raises the important question of poetic parallelism. Each of the three possible readings considered above has at some point in church history been adopted as the correct way to read the poetic line (see chapter 6). Finally, the description in Revelation of the beast rising from the sea reminds us not to ignore the possibility of metaphorical language.

I intend in this book to survey the literary nature of the Bible and to acquaint the reader with the research that is being carried out on the Bible by literary scholars. Such research is both theoretical and practical. Theorists ask questions about the nature of literary language. How does a literary text communicate to a reader? What does it communicate? Is the goal of interpretation to determine the intention of the author, or does the reader shape the meaning of the text? Or should we forget about the author and the reader and concentrate on the text alone? What is a genre? Does genre even exist? How do prose and poetry differ? Does truly literal language exist, or is all language metaphorical? On the other hand, literary research may be practical—that is, applicable to actual texts. What is the genre of Ecclesiastes? Are repetitions in the patriarchal narratives signs of multiple sources, or do they reflect conventions of ancient Hebrew storytelling?

The theory of literary criticism and its practice are, of course, not isolated from one another. One must have a theory of genre before asking about the genre of a particular text. At the same time, one must work with particular texts and see similarities between them before formulating a theory of genre. Nevertheless, such a division between theory and application is useful and underlies the two-part division of this book.

Various schools of thought have arisen in the field of secular literary theory, and it is not surprising that these differences are reflected in biblical studies. In the secondary literature we frequently encounter titles that begin "A Semiotic Approach to" or "A Structuralist Understanding of"; even the word *deconstruction* has been creeping into the literature. Technical terminology peppers the pages of contemporary journal articles—narratology, *signifié,* binary opposition, *langue/parole,* actant. The first chapter serves as a guide to the interaction between secular literary theory and biblical studies and attempts to bring some order out of the chaos of the many different approaches.

Chapter 2 then analyzes and evaluates the trends of modern literary criticism, particularly as applied to biblical studies. The pitfalls and promises of a literary approach for biblical studies will be highlighted. Certainly the most urgent of the potential pitfalls is the relationship between literature and history. Can the Bible, particularly if it is literature, make meaningful historical statements? In other words, does the Bible contain history or story? Conservative as well as traditional critical scholars have assumed that the Bible intends to make statements about history. (They disagree, however, about the accuracy of the history.) On the other hand, many advocates of literary criticism agree with D. Robertson that "nothing depends on the truth or falsity of [the Bible's] historical claims."[1]

The third chapter closes this first part with a brief summary of the method I advocate in this book. I seek an approach that is low on jargon and high on results in exegesis.

The practice of literary criticism is the focus of part 2. What tools, methods, and insights have been developed from the literary approach that are particularly helpful in understanding specific texts? Chapter 4 concerns prose narrative, and chapter 6 deals with poetry. Chapters 5 and 7 provide examples of the analysis of prose and poetry respectively. A short epilogue closes the discussion.

To use terminology popularized by Jonathan Culler, I seek to make readers conversant with the "enabling conventions" of prose and poetry and thus to encourage competence in reading biblical literature.[2] As we will see, writings are not created out of whole cloth but, rather, use the familiar forms of previous writings in order to communicate with the reader. The writer sends signals to the reader in order to instruct him or her regarding how to understand the message.

To learn the conventions of Old and New Testament literature is to take steps toward becoming a competent interpreter. When Culler speaks of competency in literature, he treats literature like language and borrows from linguistics. When a student becomes competent in a foreign language, it does not mean that he or she knows every word of, say, German, and can translate at sight any sentence encountered. It means rather that the student knows the basic rules of syntax and how to use a dictionary. Literature is similar to syntax and the interpretation of sentences, in that to know the rules is the first step toward understanding any particular text.

From many different quarters the claim is going out that biblical studies are undergoing a paradigm shift.[3] The literary

---

[1] D. Robertson, "Literature, the Bible as," *IDB* Supplementary Volume, p. 548.

[2] J. Culler, *Structuralist Poetics* (Ithaca: Cornell, 1975), pp. 113–60.

[3] J. D. Crossan, " 'Ruth Amid the Alien Corn': Perspectives and Methods in Contemporary Biblical Criticism," in *The Biblical Mosaic* (ed. R. Polzin and E.

approach is heralded as an innovation in interpretation and not simply another tool comparable to source, form, or redaction criticism. Indeed some of the more radical proponents of the approach downplay traditional approaches: "Literary critics in general do not believe it is necessary to use the traditional disciplines of biblical research or to employ the findings of those disciplines."[4] A good example of this attitude is found in the work of M. Weiss, who contrasts his "total interpretation" with traditional critical methods, in particular form criticism.[5] Believing that history is important to the critical understanding of a text, traditional critics have been increasingly opposed to the views of literary critics, who may be characterized as ahistorical in their approach.[6] As a result of these objections, it is common to find literary critics who acknowledge that the traditional methods are still important. This admission, however, often goes no further than lip service.

The center of the claim that literary criticism is an entirely new approach to interpretation (and also the point of disagreement with traditional approaches) is the contention that biblical texts should be studied as wholes. This view of literary criticism contrasts with the approach of form criticism, for example, because the latter emphasizes the division of a text into its constituent parts.

The following examples will demonstrate the genuine difference in mind-set between traditional criticism and literary criticism. A traditional critic discerns different sources that were brought together to constitute the Joseph narrative. Doublets are taken as evidence of a composite text. E. A. Speiser's comments on Genesis 37 are representative:

Rothman (Philadelphia: Fortress, 1982), p. 199; see also M. Fishbane, "Recent Work on Biblical Narrative," *Prooftexts* 1 (1981): 99.

[4] Robertson, "Literature," p. 548.

[5] M. Weiss, *The Bible from Within: The Method of Total Interpretation* (Jerusalem: Magnes, 1984), pp. 1–46.

[6] The tension between traditional critics and literary critics has been mapped out in part by S. A. Geller, "Through Windows and Mirrors into the Bible: History, Literature, and Language in the Study of Text," in *A Sense of Text* (*JQRS*, 1982): 3–40.

> The narrative is broken up into two originally independent versions. One of these (J) used the name Israel, featured Judah as Joseph's protector, and identified the Ishmaelites as the traders who bought Joseph from his brothers. The other (E) spoke of Jacob as the father and named Reuben as Joseph's friend; the slave traders in that version were Midianites who discovered Joseph by accident and sold him in Egypt to Potiphar.[7]

For Speiser, two stories similar in details and structure signal two different sources. For the literary critic, on the other hand, the issue of sources is irrelevant. There may or may not be different sources; the important matter is the shape of the text as it is before us. Narrative style, not a conflation of sources, explains the doublets. (The approach displays a family resemblance with canonical criticism.)[8]

Such an approach to Genesis 37 may be found in Adele Berlin's helpful book *Poetics and Interpretation of Biblical Narrative*. She sets her analysis over against traditional source criticism and concludes, "On the basis of plot and discourse, the present text is a unified product. . . . To be sure, there are gaps, inconsistencies, retellings, and changes in vocabulary in biblical narrative, but these can be viewed as part of a literary technique and are not necessarily signs of different sources."[9]

The flood story also illustrates the emphasis of traditional criticism on discovering sources rather than interpreting whole texts. Scholars often divide Genesis 6:5–8:22 into two sources, P and a second source usually identified as J. The tendency of traditional criticism is to highlight apparent discrepancies and to attribute repetition to different sources.[10]

G. J. Wenham, on the other hand, examined this text as a whole and discovered that the flood account was very carefully

---

[7] E. A. Speiser, *Genesis* (Anchor Bible 1; Garden City, N.Y.: Doubleday, 1964), pp. 293–94.

[8] J. Barton, *Reading the Old Testament* (Philadelphia: Westminster, 1984), pp. 77–88.

[9] A. Berlin, *Poetics and Interpretation of Biblical Narrative* (Sheffield: Almond, 1983), p. 121.

[10] See, for instance, G. von Rad, *Genesis* (Philadelphia: Westminster, 1972), pp. 119–21; Speiser, *Genesis* pp. 54–56.

and tightly structured. He was able to identify the structure as a chiasm (see chapter 7). His conclusion was that "Genesis vi–ix is a carefully composed piece of literature, which is more coherent than usually admitted. . . . The Genesis flood story is a coherent narrative within the conventions of Hebrew story-telling."[11]

Up to this point we have been speaking of literary approaches or literary criticism. This terminology is appropriate because it makes explicit the connection with nonbiblical literary criticism. As with other approaches, notably the sociological approach, literary criticism is highly interdiscipli-nary.[12] While biblical studies has had contact with secular literary studies for centuries (see chapter 1), until recently there has been only sporadic interaction. Within the last two decades biblical studies has become much more conscious of the need to understand and employ the concepts and tools of literary analysis. Biblical scholars have turned to literary study for help (Polzin, Detweiler, Crossan, Via, etc.), and an increasing number of literary scholars have turned to the Bible as an object of study (Alter, Kermode, Ryken, Frye). Such interests have led to the rise of the literary approach in biblical studies, most commonly referred to as literary criticism.

The terminology may lead to confusion. The term *literary criticism* already has a specialized meaning in biblical studies, wherein it most commonly refers to source criticism. Due to the possibility of confusion, some have advocated the use of the term *aesthetic criticism* to describe the literary approach. Others desire to broaden the scope of *rhetorical criticism,* though it usually refers only to matters of style. Both terms, however, are too narrow for our purposes. In the literary approach, we are interested in more than the study of beauty and people's response to it. We are interested in more than the study of style, or those "artistic means (in a text) for achieving effects upon the

---

[11]G. J. Wenham, "The Coherence of the Flood Narrative," *VT* 28 (1978): 337, 347.

[12]For a good introduction to the sociological method, see R. R. Wilson, *Sociological Approaches to the Old Testament* (Philadelphia: Fortress, 1984).

reader or audience."[13] In the final analysis, *literary criticism,* in spite of ambiguity and possible confusion, is the best term to describe the type of analysis outlined in this book. Before going further, however, it is necessary to answer a few basic questions. What is literature? What is the literary approach? Is the Bible literature?

Some scholars and even more laypeople understandably object to the idea of a literary approach. It appears to reduce the Scriptures to the level of the classics or, worse than that, to equate the Bible with imaginative or fictional writing. Many are acquainted with a literary approach through high-school courses entitled "The Bible as Literature." Such a title connotes a supposedly neutral or nonreligious approach to the text, thus making it a "safe" course for state-supported schools. In short, the literary approach appears to reduce the Bible to something less than it is.

Scholars from many different theological stripes may be cited warning us against the dangers implicit in such an approach:

> There is something artificial in the idea of "the Bible as 'literature.'" Or rather, it can be artificial and contrary to the perception of both most believers and most unbelievers. (K. Stendahl)

> Those who talk of reading the Bible "as literature" sometimes mean, I think, reading it without attending to the main thing it is about. (C. S. Lewis)

> Whoever turns a gospel of Christ into a novel has wounded my heart. (J. G. Herder)

> The persons who enjoy these writings solely because of their literary merit are essentially parasites; and we know that parasites, when they become too numerous, are pests. I could easily fulminate for a whole hour against the men of letters who have gone into ecstasies over "the Bible as literature." (T. S. Eliot)[14]

---

[13]M. H. Abrams, *A Glossary of Literary Terms,* 4th ed. (New York: Holt, Rinehart & Winston, 1981), p. 160.

[14]K. Stendahl, "The Bible as a Classic and the Bible as Holy Scripture," *JBL* 103 (1984): 6; C. S. Lewis, *Reflections on the Psalms* (Glasgow: Collins, 1961),

The danger of reducing the Bible to the level of a good story without grounding in actual events and without impact in the real world is a real danger. The issue is simply what it means to "treat the Bible as literature."

The question "What is literature?" is not an easy one. Many answers have been proposed. Some have suggested that everything in print is literature.[15] Most scholars, however, argue that literature is a subset of written texts. According to the popular textbook *Theory of Literature,* "The term 'literature' seems best if we limit it to the art of literature, that is, to imaginative literature. . . . We recognize 'fictionality,' 'invention,' or 'imagination' as the distinguishing trait of literature."[16] The full implications of adopting a similar view of the Bible will be discussed in chapter 2. For now, however, it is necessary simply to state that a literary approach to the study of Scriptures does not imply, as some might think, a belief that the Bible as a whole is story, not history, or that it speaks of another world and not the real world of time and space.

A literary approach to the Bible is possible because its texts are obviously self-conscious about form. Artful verbal expression is frequently encountered in the Old and New Testaments.[17] This attention to the verbal texture makes the Bible at least in great part amenable to a literary approach. C. S. Lewis qualifies his negative assessment (quoted above) about a literary approach by saying, "But there is a saner sense in which the Bible, since it is after all literature, cannot properly be read except as literature; and the different parts of it as the different sorts of literature they are."[18] Northrup Frye has well stated, "The Bible is as literary as it can well be without actually being

p. 10; J. G. Herder, quoted in F. Kermode, *The Genesis of Secrecy* (Cambridge: Harvard University Press, 1979), p. 120; T. S. Eliot, *Essays, Ancient and Modern* (London, 1936), p. 95.

[15] C. Di Girolamo, *A Critical Theory of Literature* (Madison: University of Wisconsin Press, 1981).

[16] R. Wellek and A. Warren, *Theory of Literature,* 3d ed. (New York: Harcourt Brace Jovanovich, 1977), pp. 22, 26.

[17] Berlin, *Poetics and Interpretation,* esp. chap. 6, "The Art of Biblical Narrative."

[18] Lewis, *Psalms,* p. 10.

literature."[19] Of course, the Bible is not uniformly literary. Poetry as a whole is certainly a more self-conscious use of language than prose, though Robert Alter (see chapter 4) has forcefully demonstrated that prose is artful in its composition.[20] A second problem inherent in the proposed approach to the Scriptures as literature is the vagueness of the phrase "artful verbal expression." What is literariness? Literary language is frequently defined by contrast with everyday language, but Di Girolamo and others have shown the immense difficulties of precision in such distinctions, and McKnight's position that texts are literary only when they are read as literature is not helpful.[21]

Nonetheless, such careful distinctions are not necessary to demonstrate the self-consciousness of biblical language. The descriptions of story structures and poetic devices are enough to show that literary concepts and tools are useful in the exegesis of biblical texts. Such descriptions will be given in chapters 4 and 6.

We begin now in part 1 by reviewing some aspects of the theory behind the literary approach to the Bible. Such a study will prepare the way for the analysis of seven specific texts in part 2.

---

[19]N. Frye, *The Great Code* (London: Ark, 1982), p. 62.

[20]R. Alter, *The Art of Biblical Narrative* (New York: Basic Books, 1981), pp. 3–22.

[21]Di Girolamo, *Critical Theory*, pp. 13–20; E. McKnight, *The Bible and the Reader: An Introduction to Literary Criticism* (Philadelphia: Fortress, 1985), pp. 9–11.

Part 1

THEORY

1

A HISTORICAL SURVEY

A literary approach to the study of the Bible is both a new and an old phenomenon. In the past two decades unprecedented attention has been directed to the literary qualities of the text. In the glare of the present explosion of interest, however, we must not lose sight of the long prehistory of literary approaches. The present chapter surveys the history of the interrelationship of biblical and literary studies. The early history is lightly treated, not to denigrate its importance, but by choice our focus is the different contemporary manifestations of the literary approach. It is appropriate to emphasize the recent past, given the current fascination of the biblical scholar for the literary approach.

The chapter is not exhaustive but serves as a beginning guide to the use of literary concepts and tools in the field of biblical studies. The concentration in the historical survey will clearly be on the second half of the twentieth century. Pre-twentieth-century schools and figures chosen for comment are cited as high points or representatives.

PRECURSORS TO THE LITERARY APPROACH

Patristic Interpretation

Many of the early church fathers were educated in classical rhetoric and poetics. As a result, they frequently applied the principles of literature that they learned in school to the study of the Scriptures. They often compared biblical stories and poems with ones familiar to them in classical literature. The result was, from a modern perspective, a distortion of understanding and evaluation of the biblical texts. Jerome, for example, scanned Hebrew poems and described their poetic form in labels developed for Greek and Latin poetry.[1] Kugel quotes Jerome as saying:

> What is more musical than the Psalter? which, in the manner of our Flaccus or of the Greek Pindar, now flows in iambs, now rings with Alcaics, swells to a Sapphic measure or moves along with a half-foot? What is fairer than the hymns of Deuteronomy or Isaiah? What is more solemn than Solomon, what more polished than Job? All of which books, as Josephus and Origen write, flow in the original in hexameter and pentameter verses.[2]

Augustine too compared biblical stories with classical stories and found the former rough and clumsy in their form when compared with the latter. In his *Confessions* (Book 3:5) we find the following telling comment:

> So I made up my mind to examine the holy Scriptures and see what kind of books they were. I discovered something that was at once beyond the understanding of the proud and hidden from the eyes of children. Its gait was humble, but the heights it reached were sublime. . . . When I first looked into the Scriptures . . . they seemed quite unworthy of comparison with the stately prose of Cicero.[3]

Augustine thought that the Bible had a low literary quality, which for him represented a test of faith and humility. The intellectual must be willing to accept the idea that the Bible is inferior literature and must still believe the message. Other fathers of the church attempted to prove that the Bible was actually superior to pagan literature in its form as well as in its content.

---

[1] J. Kugel, *The Idea of Biblical Poetry* (New Haven: Yale University Press, 1981), pp. 149–56.

[2] Ibid., p. 152.

[3] Quoted in ibid., pp. 159–60.

Of course, the flaw inherent in the Fathers' literary approach to the Bible is that they judged the text by standards developed for the analysis of a foreign literature. The imposition of alien values on the biblical text is a pitfall that continues to the present day (see chapter 2). The positive aspect of the Fathers' approach is that they recognized the literary qualities of the biblical stories, an awareness that gradually diminished as the content of the Scriptures was abstracted into various theological systems.

Robert Lowth and the Study of Hebrew Poetry

Poetry is so obviously literary, in the sense of artful and conventional, that it was subjected to literary analysis long before prose. Robert Lowth, who was a professor of English at Oxford in the late eighteenth century, wrote a landmark analysis of the workings of Hebrew poetry, particularly parallelism.[4] By categorizing parallelism, discussing meter, and describing other poetic devices, Lowth approached part of the Bible as a literary text. He was, in essence, describing the conventions that shaped the writing of the Psalms, Isaiah, and other poetic texts. Lowth's results, though eventually receiving considerable modification, aided in the correct reading of the poetry of the Old Testament.

Work on understanding the conventions and devices of Hebrew poetry has continued unabated ever since. Primarily, scholars have further refined Lowth's categories of parallelism and have suggested various schemes for describing meter. Interesting work has also been done in the area of grammatical parallelism and in the delineation of other secondary devices (see chapter 6).

Hermann Gunkel

In reading the most recent research on the literary method, one would be surprised to find Hermann Gunkel's name in a list

---

[4]R. Lowth, *Lectures on the Sacred Poetry of the Hebrews* (London: T. Tegg & Son, 1835; orig. 1753); cf. A. Baker, "Parallelism: England's Contribution to Biblical Studies," *CBQ* 35 (1973): 429–40.

of representative early developers of the literary approach. Indeed, in the eyes of some, Gunkel is the archenemy of a literary approach.[5] With his interest in discovering the individual forms and their setting in life, the emphasis was on individual texts outside of their canonical context and on a sociological rather than a literary explanation of their origins.

A definite gulf exists between Gunkel and contemporary aesthetic critics, but we should still recognize that Gunkel developed his understanding of form criticism in an interdisciplinary context. His use of the concepts of genre (*Gattung*), form (*Form*), and setting in life (*Sitz im Leben*) are heavily informed by literary and sociological theories of his day.[6] Indeed one of the difficulties with biblical form criticism as traditionally practiced is not that it is aliterary in its understanding of genre but that it adopts a neoclassical concept of genre that was obsolete even in Gunkel's day.[7] In any case, Gunkel advanced a literary approach to the study of Scripture by focusing attention on the all-important issue of identifying the genre of a text in the process of interpretation.

James Muilenburg and Rhetorical Criticism

James Muilenburg delivered his presidential address to the Society of Biblical Literature in 1968, an event that has since become a touchstone for holistic and literary approaches to the study of the Bible.[8] The title, "Form Criticism and Beyond," is instructive because, while appreciating the strengths of form criticism, he felt it was time to move beyond the impasse that had resulted from concentrating on individual pericopes within

---

[5] For instance, Weiss, *The Bible from Within*.

[6] G. Tucker, *Form Criticism of the Old Testament* (Philadelphia: Fortress, 1971), pp. 4–5; and M. J. Buss, "The Study of Forms," in *Old Testament Form Criticism*, ed. J. H. Mayes (San Antonio: Trinity University Press, 1974), p. 50.

[7] Neo-classical genre theory is a nineteenth-century phenomenon that held a rigid view of genres as pure and hierarchical; see G. N. G. Orsini, "Genres," in *The Princeton Encyclopedia of Poetry and Poetics* (Princeton: Princeton University Press, 1974), p. 308.

[8] J. Muilenburg, "Form Criticism and Beyond," *JBL* 88 (1969): 1–18.

texts. He was concerned as well with the emphasis that form criticism placed on the "typical and representative" to the exclusion of "individual, personal, and unique features." On the positive side, he recognized that the Old Testament had a high literary quality and promoted the study of style. His work has since stimulated many other studies connected with the style of Hebrew poetry and prose.

The preceding survey is very schematic. It completely ignores some major figures of the past, particularly the medieval period and also of this century (Norden, König, and Alonso-Schökel, for instance). Nonetheless, it is now clear that the modern literary approach has a long history in the field of biblical interpretation, even if it has never before reached the current level of activity.

As we now turn to the modern period of literary study of the Bible, there are many ways in which we could proceed. One possible approach is chronological and charts the different dominant schools of thought in secular literary study and then gives examples concerning how each school of thought has exerted an influence on biblical studies. To proceed in such a way, one would begin with New Criticism, then consider structuralism and semiotics, and finally conclude with deconstruction. Other influential minority positions could then be discussed, particularly reader-response, archetypal, Marxist, and feminist literary criticism.

Biblical studies, however, does not follow the chronological pattern of secular theory. Some researchers in Bible write in a New Critical mode long after New Criticism has passed away as a major school in literary theory. Others adopt more traditional modes of literary criticism, even in this age of deconstruction. In reality, of course, this diversity reflects the situation in literary theory. Deconstruction may be the avant-garde movement today, but many in literary theory either blithely or studiously avoid it in order to continue in traditional, perhaps even pre-New Critical, modes of interpretation.[9]

---

[9] Some believe, however, that deconstruction is already somewhat passé, evidence for which they see in an article by C. Campbell, "The Tyranny of the Yale Critics," *New York Times Magazine*, Feb. 9, 1986.

Instead of a diachronic survey of literary theory, then, I employ a synchronic analysis.

Each school of thought concentrates attention on one element of what might be called the act of literary communication. A literary text may be seen as a message of one sort or another addressed by an author to a reader. The communication itself takes place in a certain social and temporal context, which may be called the universe. These relations may be diagramed as follows:

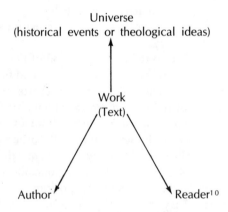

Universe
(historical events or theological ideas)

Work
(Text)

Author   Reader[10]

Theorists of the traditional school believe that we should interpret the meaning of a piece of literature by concentrating on the author. Others focus on the text, and still others focus on the reader. I discuss the various schools of literary theory under their respective focuses—author-centered, text-centered, and reader-centered. The main principles of each school of literary study will be examined, followed by specific examples of the influence each has exercised on biblical studies.

[10] M. H. Abrams, *The Mirror and the Lamp* (New York: Oxford University Press, 1953), pp. 3–29; and J. Barton, "Classifying Biblical Criticism," *JSOT* 29 (1984): 19–35.

AUTHOR-CENTERED THEORIES

Literary Studies

Modern literary criticism has rejected the author as the major element in the interpretive process. Since the advent of New Criticism in the 1940s until the present, theorists have proclaimed the death of the author, granting authors no privileged insight into their own work. This trend, of course, is a complete reversal of the traditional approach to interpretation as it was known in the first half of the century.

TRADITIONAL CRITICISM

Traditional criticism before 1940 took great interest in the author. The key to interpretation was thought to lie in a knowledge of the activities and thought life of the author as he or she was writing a poem or narrative. The interpreter desired to discover the author's intentional meaning. Sandra Bermann describes the attitude of traditional criticism in the following illustrative way: "If we read histories, biographies, and Keats' own letters with enough scholarly patience and skill, we could be confident of 'getting the poem right,' 'understanding it,' 'interpreting its truth.' "[11] It is pivotal to know, for example, that Keats wrote his sonnet "Bright Star," with its themes of love and death, as he was caring for his brother Tom, who was dying of tuberculosis (and infecting John), and also that he was sobered by the reality of death in his passion for Fanny. This background knowledge, it was thought, provided the key to the interpretation of "Bright Star," with its lines such as the following: "I have two luxuries to brood over in my walks, your Loveliness and the hour of my death. O that I could have possession of them both in the same minute."

There are powerful arguments against such approaches. How is it possible to reconstruct an author's intention in a literary work, since he or she may not even have been conscious of it? The poet often is his or her own worst interpreter. How

---

[11] S. Bermann, "Revolution in Literary Criticism," *Princeton Alumni Weekly,* Nov. 21, 1984, p. 10.

can we get back into the mind of the poet? The latter is a problem obviously heightened in the study of an ancient text.

As discussed below, the New Critics of the forties and fifties moved away from authorial intent, a view formalized by Wimsatt and Beardsley in their description of the "intentional fallacy" and their concomitant focus on the text alone in their own interpretive strategy.[12] The intentional fallacy may be defined as a view that:

> claimed that whether the author has expressly stated what his intention was in writing a poem, or whether it is merely inferred from what we know about his life and opinions, his intention is irrelevant to the literary critic, because meaning and value reside within the text of the finished, free-standing, and public work of literature itself.[13]

Certainly the argument of the intentional fallacy has some measure of validity. Traditional critics spent so much time discussing the life and habits of authors that they lost sight of the text before them. The New Critics did a great service, as we will see, in directing attention to the text itself in the interpretive process.

E. D. HIRSCH

It is dangerous, however, to move completely away from any consideration of authorial intention, which is the decided direction of contemporary literary theory. E. D. Hirsch is an important contemporary advocate for the importance of the author.[14] Hirsch maintains that to lose sight of the author's intention in writing a text will result in the loss of any established meaning of a text. The author's intention provides a kind of anchor in the sea of interpretive relativity. For Hirsch,

---

[12] W. K. Wimsatt and M. Beardsley, "The Intentional Fallacy," reprinted in *The Verbal Icon: Studies in the Meaning of Poetry* (University Press of Kentucky, 1954), pp. 3–18. Some leading New Critics softened their view on intention later.

[13] Abrams, *Glossary*, p. 83.

[14] E. D. Hirsch, Jr., *Validity in Interpretation* (New Haven: Yale University Press, 1967); and idem, *The Aims of Interpretation* (Chicago: University of Chicago Press, 1976).

the meaning of a text is to be identified with the author's intended purpose. He is aware of all of the methodological difficulties associated with his position, notably the problem of recovering with certainty an author's purpose. After all, authors are usually not very explicit in literary works.

Hirsch's approach is interesting in that he approaches the author's meaning through a study of the text itself, particularly its genre. In other words, he infers the author's meaning primarily through a careful study of the text in relationship to other closely related texts. This move is important and approaches the balanced view that I advocate in chapter 3 below. Furthermore, Hirsch does not completely ignore the role of the reader in interpretation. He does not accept certain reader-response theories that argue that readers create meaning. Nevertheless, he does recognize that different readers will draw out different implications from the same text. He makes a distinction at this point between "meaning" and "significance." We have already seen that meaning is to be related to the author's intention. "Significance" of a literary work refers to the application that readers draw on the basis of their own background and interests.

Biblical Studies

While much of importance separates them, both critical and evangelical interpretation traditionally have focused on the author. The former has developed critical tools to enable the interpreter to go behind the final form of the text to its original setting, and the latter spends much energy on fixing and describing the time period in which the author wrote. If the author is known by name, then biographical information is utilized in interpretation.

HISTORICAL-CRITICAL METHOD

Traditional criticism, also referred to as the historical-critical method, is usually contrasted with a literary approach. As pointed out in the introduction, historical critics and literary critics often define their positions as conflicting with each other.

On another level, however, traditional criticism is a type of literary approach. It bears some resemblance to pre-New Critical approaches that seek the meaning of a text in the light of a knowledge of the author and the author's background. In biblical studies this orientation manifests itself in the concern to interpret a text in the light of its *original* setting.

The difference between traditional literary theory and traditional biblical criticism against contemporary forms of both is the difference between a diachronic and a synchronic approach. Roughly speaking a diachronic approach to literature examines the historical development of literature and is concerned with changes over time. On the other hand, a synchronic approach concentrates on one stage (usually the final form of the text), regardless of its prehistory.

Traditional critics developed tools for the study of the biblical text that were intended to recover the history of the text's development. They wanted to recover the original text and its setting. Explicitly or implicitly, these critics made the assumption that the meaning resides in its origin and has been distorted by its use in later forms. The tools most commonly associated with traditional criticism are source, form, and redaction criticism. Much could be written about each of these approaches, but for the purposes of this chapter, brief descriptions will be given. The interested reader may refer to the secondary literature cited in the footnotes.

No one has ever doubted that biblical authors utilized sources in the composition of certain books.[15] The author/editor of the books of Kings actually cites certain documents. At the end of the nineteenth century, however, hypothetical sources became the object of intense scrutiny. Source criticism of the Pentateuch came into its own primarily under the influence of Julius Wellhausen.[16] Since that time, the main

---

[15] Barton, *Reading the Old Testament,* pp. 1–29; N. Habel, *Literary Criticism of the Old Testament* (Philadelphia: Fortress, 1971); R. E. Clements, *One Hundred Years of Old Testament Interpretation* (Philadelphia: Westminster, 1976).

[16] J. Wellhausen, *Geschichte Israels I* (Marburg, 1878); 2d ed., *Prolegomena zur Geschichte Israels* (1883; Eng. trans., *Prolegomena to the History of Israel,* 1885). See

impetus in Pentateuchal studies has been the delineation, description, and dating of the various preexisting sources that make up the Torah. Source criticism is not restricted to the Pentateuch, but it began in earnest in this portion of Scripture. Use of different divine names, doublets, and other types of repetition and supposed contradictions are some of the criteria used to distinguish one source from another. The result of the study of sources is to move away from the final form of the text to its prehistory. The method is thus diachronic. Furthermore, it fragments the final form of the text into a number of sources. Both of these tendencies are resisted by modern literary approaches to the study of the Bible. It is not surprising that the modern tendency in Pentateuchal studies is to move away from source analysis.[17]

Form criticism developed partly in reaction to source criticism, though it does not necessarily conflict with it.[18] As formulated by Gunkel and others, form criticism too is a diachronic method, seeking to discover the *original* form and setting of a particular biblical passage. The implicit assumption is that the key to the meaning of a passage is located in its original use and not in its final (distorted) form. Form criticism studies a text in the light of other texts that are similar in terms of structure, content, language, and so forth. Gunkel argued that each form had one and only one setting and that that setting was a sociological one. Sigmund Mowinckel, a student of Gunkel's, argued, for instance, that the Psalms for the most part found their original home in an annual enthronement festival.

The next logical step is redaction criticism.[19] Once again it is partly a reaction against its past—in this case, form criticism.

---

now J. Rogerson, *Old Testament Criticism in the Nineteenth Century: England and Germany* (Philadelphia: Fortress, 1985).

[17] I. M. Kikawada and A. Quinn, *Before Abraham Was: The Unity of Genesis 1–11* (Nashville: Abingdon, 1985).

[18] Barton, *Reading the Old Testament,* pp. 30–44; Tucker, *Form Criticism;* for a more detailed discussion and fuller bibliography, see my "Form Criticism, Recent Developments in Genre Theory and the Evangelical," *WTJ* 47 (1985): 46–67.

[19] Barton, *Reading the Old Testament,* pp. 45–76; J. A. Wharton, "Redaction Criticism, Old Testament," *IDB,* Supplementary Volume, 729–32.

Form criticism tended to fragment a text. The concern was to *isolate* a passage from its context in the biblical text and study it in the light of its prehistory. Redaction criticism deals with the shape of the final form. What principles were active in the bringing together of these isolated forms? This approach usually tries to identify the theological concerns of the redactor, or editor, the so-called *Tendenz*. Redaction criticism is obviously helpful in the study of the Gospels or Kings and Chronicles, where the same events are being presented two or more times. It becomes much more tentative where there is no parallel text to serve as a control. Redaction criticism is a step beyond both source and form criticism in looking for the hand that drew the text into its final form. With redaction criticism we are moving closer to what we recognize as contemporary literary criticism with its interest on the final form of the text.

These brief descriptions of source, form, and redaction criticism show a contrast with the agenda of modern literary approaches. The difference may be summarized as the difference between a diachronic and a synchronic approach. The diachronic approach asks questions that are extrinsic to the text itself: Who is the author? What are the author's characteristics? What is the historical background of the text? and so forth. Implicitly or explicitly, the interpretive key is thought to lie outside of the text itself in its origin or background. These questions still arise in literary theory, but the approach to literature that they imply is now recognized as obsolete or problematic. Advocates of a literary approach tend to reject, ignore, or seriously modify these tools of historical criticism. Recently, however, there have been attempts at synthesis.[20]

TRADITIONAL EVANGELICAL APPROACHES

Evangelicals, for the most part, have also assumed that the meaning of a text resides in the author's intention and the historical background. The *historical*-grammatical approach to interpretation has emphasized the need to study the Bible in the

---

[20] V. Philips Longs, "The Reign and Rejection of King Saul" (Ph.D. diss., Cambridge University, 1987).

light of its historical origin. Of course, the major difference with traditional critical approaches is that the text has been identified with its canonical form, the final form of the text. A recent, lucid defense of identifying the meaning of a text with the author's intention is that of Walter Kaiser. Kaiser applied the theory of E. D. Hirsch to the situation of biblical exegesis and boldly stated, "The *author's* intended meaning is what a text means."[21]

TEXT-CENTERED THEORIES

Literary Studies

Extreme cases of the traditional approach studied everything but the work of literature itself. The reaction came in the 1940s and continues until the present day. Critics have shifted dramatically from a study of the origin and development of a piece of literature to a study of the text itself. Since text-oriented theories focus on the poem or prose narrative, they are collectively referred to as an objective theory of interpretation as opposed to a mimetic or expressive theory.[22] Two major schools of thought will be presented at this point: New Criticism and structuralism.

NEW CRITICISM

New Criticism describes a general trend in literary theory that dominated thinking in the 1940s and 1950s. While many differences of opinion existed among the various scholars identified with this school of thought, they were united on the major points discussed below. Cleanth Brooks, Robert Penn Warren, and W. K. Wimsatt in the United States and F. R. Leavis in Britain are a few of the prominent scholars usually associated with New Criticism. The roots of the movement, however, may be traced to the thought of T. S. Eliot, I. A. Richards, and W. Empson. The name may be traced to the title

[21] W. Kaiser, *Toward an Exegetical Theology* (Grand Rapids: Baker, 1981), p. 33.

[22] For this terminology, see Barton, "Classifying."

of John Crowe Ransom's book *The New Criticism,* published in 1941. Many of the concerns of this predominantly Anglo-American school are shared by Russian formalism, but discussion of this latter school will be delayed until later, since there is a direct connection with structuralism.

The primary tenet of New Criticism may be expressed positively and negatively: the literary work is self-sufficient; the author's intention and background are unimportant to the critic. New Critics speak of the literary text as an artifact or verbal icon. Both of these metaphors express the self-sufficiency of the literary work. Such critics require (indeed must restrict themselves to) only the text and do not use outside, or extrinsic, information in its interpretation. The self-sufficiency of the literary text implies the denial of the author. The author does not speak from a position of privilege or special insight into his or her own text. Here, New Criticism parts company with traditional interpretation, not only of the first part of this century, but since the Enlightenment.

The self-sufficiency of the text further implies the necessity for a close reading of the text. If meaning resides in the text itself, it may be discovered only through careful analysis. Such close reading analyzes the complex interrelationships within the work itself. The study of poetic ambiguity (in the sense of multiple meaning), tension, irony, and paradox are examples of the literary concerns of New Critical scholars.

In the late 1950s New Criticism faded as the dominant force in literary studies.[23] Until that time the ideas associated with New Criticism were widespread, being taught even on the high-school level. It is not surprising, therefore, that its influence was felt on biblical studies as well. M. Weiss, for example, explicitly states and applies the principles of New Criticism to the interpretation of the biblical text.[24] Weiss cites various New Critical theories to justify his rejection of external approaches to the meaning of a passage of Scripture and to read the text "closely." He is concerned with the interpretation of

---

[23] F. Lentricchia, *After the New Criticism* (London: Methuen, 1980), p. 4.
[24] Weiss, *The Bible from Within.*

the whole poem as it stands, thus the name *total interpretation* for his approach. His book begins with studies of texts on the word and phrase levels. He continues with an analysis of sentences and sequences of sentences and then concludes with research on structure and whole texts. The outline of his book illustrates his twin concerns with close reading and with the text as a whole.

The "Sheffield school" and those more or less associated with it (mostly through the *Journal for the Study of the Old Testament*) have in the past adopted many of New Criticism's insights into biblical exegesis. Good examples may be cited in D. Gunn's stimulating studies of the Saul and David materials.[25] See also A. Berlin's work.[26]

J. Barton has advanced the provocative thesis that B. Childs's "canonical method" is formally related to New Criticism.[27] Childs himself, Barton concedes, distances himself from any literary justification for his approach. Nonetheless, Childs's treatment of biblical texts as self-sufficient and as understood within a literary tradition (canon) bears a close relationship to the principles of New Criticism.

STRUCTURALISM

New Criticism has had a relatively minor impact on biblical studies. In contrast, structuralism is of major importance in contemporary research on the Old and New Testaments. Structuralism describes a broad movement that affects many disciplines. Linguistics, anthropology, law, philosophy, and sociology are just a few, though perhaps the most discussed, of the fields of study in which an application of structural thinking may be found. Structuralism is broad in a second sense as well. Vastly different approaches are placed under the structuralist umbrella. As Poythress has stated, "Structuralism is more a diverse collection of methods, paradigms and personal preferences than it is a 'system,' a theory or

---

[25] D. Gunn, *The Story of King David: Genre and Interpretation* (*JSOT* Supp. 6; Sheffield: JSOT, 1978); idem, *The Fate of King Saul: An Interpretation of a Biblical Story* (*JSOT* Supp. 14; Sheffield: JSOT, 1980).

[26] Berlin, *Poetics and Interpretation*.

[27] Barton, *Reading the Old Testament*, pp. 140–57.

a well formulated thesis."[28] Most important, perhaps, structuralism is broad in that it claims to be, "not a method of inquiry, but a general theory about human culture."[29]

By necessity then, our brief description of structuralism will be simplistic. After a short history of the development of structuralism, the main principles will be displayed and discussed. The structuralism presented here might be called the conservative version, associated with the early R. Barthes and the summarizing work of J. Culler.

History of development. The linguist Ferdinand de Saussure turned the attention of his field to the sign nature of language. He is commonly credited as the father of structuralism, though a lesser-known precursor is Charles S. Peirce. Saussure, whose major work is really the posthumous compilation of his lecture notes, proposed a series of distinctions that set the stage for modern studies.[30] His most famous division is between *langue* and *parole*. The former may be defined as "a system, an institution, a set of interpersonal rules and norms."[31] The latter refers to actual sentences used in writing or speaking. The second distinction identifies the two aspects of a sign, particularly the linguistic sign: the *signifier* and the *signified*. The signifier refers to the word, or acoustical image, while the signified pertains to the concept evoked by the signifier. Consider the word *dog*. The combination of the letters themselves, or, better, the phonemes represented by the letters, are the signifier. The concept (not the object, since the dog may be a nonexistent, metaphorical dog) evoked by the signifier is an animal of a certain species. The relationship between the signifier and the signified is *arbitrary* in that there is no inherent, predetermined relationship between the acoustical image and the concept. This fact may be demonstrated easily by noting the different words used in various languages to refer to the animal English speakers call *dog*.

---

[28] V. S. Poythress, "Structuralism and Biblical Studies," *JETS* 21 (1978): 221.

[29] Barton, *Reading the Old Testament,* p. 112.

[30] F. de Saussure, *Course in General Linguistics,* ed. C. Bally and A. Sechehaye (New York: McGraw-Hill, 1959).

[31] Culler, *Structuralist Poetics,* p. 8.

A third distinction places syntagmatic analysis over against paradigmatic analysis. This distinction is illustrated most simply on the level of the sentence. In *the man saw the wolf,* a syntagmatic approach would analyze the five words in the sentence in their relationships to each other. A paradigmatic analysis, on the other hand, examines each slot in the sentence: *the man / saw / the wolf.* As McKnight states it: "Paradigmatic relationships of a word are those which may replace it in a sentence without making the sentence unacceptable."[32] These words are related as a group, and the use of any one will call into mind the others. For instance, *saw* could be replaced by *observed, espied,* or the like. This third Saussurian distinction is particularly important in differentiating the variation between Propp's and Lévi-Strauss's method of studying narrative (see below).

Meanwhile in Moscow and later in Prague, literary scholars (as a group labeled Russian formalists) were exploring avenues that eventually led to common concerns and approaches with European and American structuralists.[33] Indeed, the connection is embodied in one prominent practitioner of structuralism, Roman Jakobson. Jakobson was involved with the Moscow Linguistic Circle (founded in 1915), moved to Prague when the Moscow group was suppressed by the Soviets, and eventually ended up in New York, where he influenced the anthropologist Claude Lévi-Strauss. A second major figure of Russian formalism whose work provided a direct influence on the development of structuralist approaches to narrative is V. Propp.

Structuralism as a major school of literary criticism really began only in the 1960s. H. Felperin would date the coming of age of literary structuralism to 1966, the year in which Roland Barthes published *Critique et vérité.*[34] Here, Barthes proclaimed the importance of what he called the "science of literature,"

---

[32] McKnight, *The Bible and the Reader,* p. 7.

[33] F. Jameson, *The Prison-House of Language* (Princeton: Princeton University Press, 1972), pp. 43–98; most recently, McKnight, *The Bible and the Reader,* pp. 16–19.

[34] H. Felperin, *Beyond Deconstruction* (Oxford: Clarendon, 1985), p. 74.

which is concerned not with the interpretation of particular works but with the "conditions of meaning." He and others such as Todorov desired to describe a "grammar" of literature.

Major principles. A major impetus for the development of structuralism in the area of literary criticism was the desire to be "scientific," to raise literary studies from the realm of the subjective to the objective—that is, to provide literature with a method of analysis that could be demonstrated and repeated. As R. C. Culley summarized it, structuralists "are seeking a method which is scientific in the sense that they are striving for a rigorous statement and an exacting analytical model."[35] More recent structuralist studies do not take such a radically scientific approach.[36]

Structuralism developed from linguistics. In particular, the development traces to Saussure's insight into the nature of the sign in linguistics. Another common name for this field is semiotics (from the Greek word for *sign*). Words are perhaps the clearest examples of Saussure's thought as he discussed the workings of signs. Structuralism as a whole may be defined as the extension of the linguistic metaphor to other semiotic systems. Literature is considered by structuralists to be a "second-order semiotic system," in that literary texts are constructed from language. Literature and literary texts are, therefore, capable of structuralist analysis.

The analogy between linguistics and literature leads to insights into the nature of literature. The two most important ideas for our purposes are literary competence and literature as systemic. The conception of literary competence may be traced back to Saussure's foundational distinction between *langue* and *parole,* or abstract rules and actual utterances. Speakers of a language do not have a complete or explicit knowledge of all the rules. These rules are "tacitly shared by members of a

---

[35] R. C. Culley, "Exploring New Directions," in *The Hebrew Bible and Its Modern Interpreters,* ed. D. A. Knight and G. M. Tucker (Philadelphia: Fortress, 1985), p. 174.

[36] R. Polzin, *Biblical Structuralism* (Philadelphia: Fortress, 1977), esp. chap. 1, "What Is Structuralism?"

speech community."[37] The internalization of *langue* permits the understanding of any particular utterance. When studying a second language, for instance, the student learns the rules of morphology and syntax, memorizes basic vocabulary, and thus becomes competent in that language. Noam Chomsky popularized the notions of *competence,* which describes the mastery of the basic rules of a language, and *performance,* which concerns the production of actual sentences.[38]

Early structuralist critics extended this linguistic notion to literature. One becomes competent in a literary tradition or literature in general by learning the syntax, or rules, of narrative. Deep underlying structures may be discerned that cut across literature as a whole. Another way of describing these rules is to call them *conventions.*

Structuralists and their interpreters often illustrate these ideas by using game analogies. American football, for example, is played by a set of rules that are not too difficult to assimilate or internalize, but unless they are learned, one cannot play the game or even follow it. To become competent in football entails learning the rules and conventions of the game (i.e., a forward pass is permissible, a lineman may not go downfield on a pass play, etc.).

Literary conventions are numerous and depend on the type of literature being analyzed. Indeed, genre is a way of describing a convention of literature. The interpreter needs to distinguish between prose and poetry, novel and lyric, etc. Such an approach to literature leads to the suppression of both the author and the reader in structuralist thought. As Culler describes it: "The [structuralist] concepts of *écriture* and *lecture* have been brought to the fore so as to divert attention from the author as source and the work as object and focus it instead on two correlated networks of convention: writing as an institution and reading as an activity."[39]

To put it perhaps in extreme form, writers are not seen as

---

[37] Abrams, *Glossary,* p. 95.
[38] Culler, *Structuralist Poetics,* p. 9.
[39] Ibid., p. 131.

original contributors to their work but as users of previous devices. Their work is a conglomeration of previous works. Since, by necessity, only established literary conventions can be used, the meaning of the work is found in the convention rather than the intention of the author. The common use of literary conventions describes the structuralist notion *intertextuality*. According to Julia Kristeva, "Every text takes shape as a mosaic of citations, every text is the absorption and transformation of other texts. The notion of intertextuality comes to take the place of the notion of intersubjectivity."[40] The reader meets the same fate. The competent reader has assimilated the conventions. He or she brings nothing to the interpretation of the text besides an explicit and implicit knowledge of how literature "works." In short, the meaning of a text resides in the conventional code, which has a public meaning, not in the author's intention or in the reader's preunderstanding. Reading is a "rule-governed process."[41] According to Robert Scholes, both readers and authors are "divided psyches traversed by codes."[42]

Besides the idea of literary competence, the notion of *literature as systemic* represents a second insight provided by the structuralist analogy between linguistics and literature. The division between the conventional nature of literature and literature as a system is artificial. The system of literature is composed of the various conventions. Once again it is helpful to begin with an illustration from linguistics. Phonemes, words, and sentences have no inherent meaning. Meaning is communicated by way of contrast within a closed system. For instance, the forms *pat* and *bat* are phonologically distinguished by the difference between *p* and *b,* which is a difference between voicelessness and voice. But *p* and *b* have meaning only in the system of English phonemes and particularly in contrast to one another. On the level of the distinctive feature, we notice

---

[40] *Semiotikè: Recherches pour une sémanalyse* (Seuil, Paris, 1969), p. 146. Quoted in Culler, *Structuralist Poetics*, p. 9.

[41] Ibid., p. 241.

[42] R. Scholes, *Semiotics and Interpretation* (New Haven: Yale University Press, 1982), p. 14.

binarism, another characteristic feature of structuralism. Structuralists "look for functional oppositions in whatever material they are studying."[43] According to Barton, structuralists

> tend to argue that all structures within which meaning can be generated, whether they be linguistic, social or aesthetic, can be analyzed in terms of pairs of opposites. . . . To be able to say what meaning is to be attached to an utterance, a gesture or an object, we need to know what it is not, as well as what it is: to know from what range of possibilities it has been selected, and what was excluded when it was chosen.[44]

Rigorous structuralists argue that, like computers, the human brain perceives and processes data according to the principle of binarism.

Structuralist approaches to prose narrative. Structuralism has emphasized prose narrative over against poetry. Structuralist study of plot and character in prose stories has had a major impact on the analysis of biblical texts. I thus describe briefly the development of structuralist thinking in this area, followed by the application of structuralism to the parable of the Good Samaritan.

I restrict my survey of structuralist approaches to prose narrative to its beginnings with V. Propp and the later refinements of A. J. Greimas. To be complete, one would need to examine the later insights of R. Barthes (in his work *S/Z*), T. Todorov, and others. Space will not permit such a survey.[45] In any case, the majority of biblical studies that adopt a structuralist perspective are theoretically dependent on Propp and Greimas.

Propp's *Morphology of the Folktale* deserves to be noted as one of the major contributions of Russian formalism.[46] Propp wrote a "morphology" or "poetics" of the folktale. He analyzed the folktale as consisting of two elements: roles and

---

[43] Culler, *Structuralist Poetics,* p. 14.

[44] Barton, *Reading the Old Testament,* p. 111.

[45] See the summary (with bibliography) of McKnight, *The Bible and the Reader,* pp. 49–58.

[46] V. Propp, *Morphology of the Folktale,* 2d ed., trans. L. A. Wagner (Austin: University of Texas Press, 1968).

functions. In examining approximately a hundred Russian tales, he concluded that there was a structure to be discerned under the surface of the text. This insight led him to describe a finite number of roles and functions that surface in actual tales in different guises.

According to Propp there are seven roles, or "spheres of actions": the villain, the donor, the helper, the sought-for person and her father, the dispatcher, the hero, and the false hero. Specific characters may fill more than one of these roles in a particular folktale, but these categories exhaust the possibilities for characters.

Propp defines a function as "an act of a character, defined from the point of view of its significance for the course of the action."[47] There are thirty-one functions, according to Propp, and while not all functions occur in any one text, they always occur in the same sequence. By way of illustration, I list here the first five of Propp's functions:

1. A member of a family leaves home (*absentation*).
2. An *interdiction* is addressed to the hero.
3. There is a *violation* of the interdiction.
4. The villain makes an attempt at *reconnaissance*.
5. The villain receives information about his victim (*delivery*).

Greimas builds on Propp's analysis and refines it so that it is more manageable.[48] The refinement takes a decided turn under the influence of Lévi-Strauss.[49] Propp's analysis may be categorized as a syntagmatic approach that follows the linear sequence of the story. Lévi-Strauss adopts a paradigmatic stance that departs from the order of the story as given and probes the structure through the analysis of "schemata" that "exist simultaneously, superimposed on one another on planes with

---

[47] Ibid., 21.

[48] A. J. Greimas, *Structural Semantics: An Attempt at a Method,* trans. D. McDowell et. al. (Lincoln: University of Nebraska Press, 1984).

[49] Cf. McKnight, *The Bible and the Reader,* pp. 53–54; R. Scheiffer, "Introduction" to Greimas, *Structural Semantics.*

different levels of abstraction."[50] He is best known for his description of the oppositional character of Propp's "spheres of action." He refers to these spheres as *actants* and charts the relationship between them in a tale in the following way:

$$Sender \longrightarrow Object \longrightarrow Receiver$$
$$\uparrow$$
$$Helper \longrightarrow Subject \longleftarrow Opponent$$

The opposition in the tale occurs between the subject and the object, the sender versus the receiver, and the helper versus the opponent. By setting Propp's functions in binary opposition, Lévi-Strauss also reduces their number to twenty.

Biblical Studies

As mentioned, biblical scholars most frequently appeal to the work of Greimas to provide the theoretical basis for their structuralist study of the Bible. These scholars have particularly used his actantial model, which is only a part or one level of his analysis. Scheiffer has noted:

> Most commentators on Greimas . . . have taken Greimas's *actantial* analysis as the central feature of his semantics of discourse, and while this is not incorrect, it has the tendency to make the technique of actantial analysis the pinnacle of Greimas's pyramid rather than to position it as a structure which both crowns and supports its neighboring structures in a kind of geodesic dome.[51]

Greimas and other structuralist writers—as well as their commentators—are often unclear in their theoretical expression. Scholes finds that Greimas is "frequently crabbed and cryptic."[52] The result is that biblical scholars are at odds

---

[50]McKnight, *The Bible and the Reader,* p. 52.

[51]Scheiffer, "Introduction," p. xli.

[52]Quoted in J. D. Crossan, "Comments on the Article of Daniel Patte," *Semeia* 2 (1974): 121.

concerning the correct application of his theory to particular texts. More basic disagreement occurs regarding the value of structural analysis for the exegetical task.

These issues may be most clearly observed by referring to the essays of Patte, Crespy, Crossan, and Tannehill in *Semeia* (1974), which focus on the analysis of the parable of the Good Samaritan. Each attempts to apply Greimas's model to the parable and comes up with strikingly different results. I discuss Patte's analysis here, since it perhaps most accurately applies Greimas's model to the text.

Patte's structuralist analysis of the parable of the Good Samaritan (Luke 10:30–35) acknowledges Greimas's three structural levels—deep, superficial (intermediate), and surface—but Patte really treats only the middle level of narrative structure. Furthermore, he divides this middle level of analysis into two types: semiotic and semantic, with the strong emphasis on the latter.

The semantic narrative structure is in turn divided into "six hierarchically distinct elements" by Patte, following Greimas. They are "sequence, syntagm, utterance, actantial model, function, and actant."[53] Each of these items is briefly explained by Patte and situated in his overall method.

Patte begins his analysis of the parable by separating the sequences, which he does by analyzing the disjunctional functions (the "movements and encounters of actors") within the parable. This analysis uncovers eight sequences in the text of the parable, which transform themselves somehow (no explanation is given) into seven *lexie*.

Patte applies the actantial model of Greimas to each of the *lexie* (unlike Crossan, who develops it for the text as a whole). Since in this section I can give little more than a taste of this type of analysis, I discuss here only the model for *lexie* 6: "and bound up his wounds, pouring on oil and wine; then he set him on his own beast and brought him to an inn, and took care of

---

[53] D. Patte, "Narrative and Structure and the Good Samaritan," *Semeia* 2 (1974): 121.

him. And the next day he took out two denarii and gave them to the innkeepers. . . ." (vv. 34–35 RSV).

Applying Greimas's actantial model to this text, we note that the sender is unknown; the object is the injured man's "status as subject," that is, his recovery; and the receiver is therefore the injured man. The subject, or hero, according to Propp's terminology, is the Samaritan; the opponents are the robbers (even though they are not mentioned in this *lexie,* Patte carries them over); and the helpers include the oil, wine, donkey, money, and innkeeper.

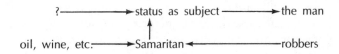

Such, in brief, is the type of analysis Patte and others use for biblical exegesis. He states that such an analysis serves the function of "reducing the narrative to its basic elements," which "clarifies what 'happens' in the text."[54] Both Crossan and Patte, however, believe that the importance of such studies really is found elsewhere in a "complete and systematic investigation of the forms and genres of the New Testament."[55] This claim has yet to be demonstrated. Perhaps, as Culley in his rather reserved praise of structuralism puts it, "Real insights are gained into the phenomenon of literature."[56] Nevertheless, its high level of complexity, its almost esoteric terminology, and its (thus far) very limited help toward understanding the text (which for many structuralists is not even a concern) have and likely will prevent the vast majority of biblical scholars from actively participating in the endeavor.

---

[54] Ibid., p. 3.
[55] Crossan, "Comments on the Article," p. 122.
[56] Culley, "Exploring," p. 177.

READER-CENTERED THEORIES

Literary Studies

So far we have surveyed theories that have placed the locus of meaning in the author and in the text. In addition, a number of recent approaches concentrate on the reader's role in the production of meaning.

Anyone who has worked with a number of students on a literary text knows that it is possible to obtain as many interpretations of the text as there are students in the class. Different readers will interpret the same text sometimes similarly, sometimes in vastly different ways. If meaning is not inherent in the author's intention or in the text itself, how are we to evaluate these different interpretations? One response is to say that they are all equally valid. Meaning resides in the reader, not in the text. The reader creates the meaning of the text.

Many reader-response theories, however, are more limited, holding that the reader *in interaction with the text* produces meaning. According to E. V. McKnight:

> The relationship between reader as subject (acting upon the text) and the reader as object (being acted upon by the text), however, is not seen as an opposition but as two sides of the same coin. It is only as the reader is subject of text and language that the reader becomes object. It is as the reader becomes object that the fullness of the reader's needs and desires as subject are met.[57]

In this view, readers are not free to do what they will with the text but are constrained by the text in their interpretation.

Who is the reader according to these theories? Differences abound. Some refer to any old reader; others have in mind a "superreader," "informed reader," "ideal reader," or, in structuralist terms, the completely competent reader.[58] We do not need to solve these problems. We simply recognize that certain theorists concentrate on the reader's role in the process of interpretation.

---

[57] McKnight, *The Bible and the Reader*, p. 128.

[58] R. M. Fowler, "Who Is 'the Reader' in Reader Response Criticism," *Semeia* 31 (1985): 5–23.

Biblical Studies

Thus far few biblical scholars have argued for an exclusively reader-response approach to exegesis. Scholars, however, are increasingly recognizing the role of the reader in interpretation. For instance, Anthony Thiselton describes the act of interpretation as a bridging of two horizons: that of the text and that of the reader. Significantly, he does not call for a complete divestment of the reader's preunderstanding as one encounters the text.[59]

The most frequent appeal to reader-response theory in biblical studies comes from those who might be called "ideological readers." Here I refer to those who read the Scriptures with a definite, usually political, agenda. The two most prominent types of ideological readers today are liberation theologians and feminist scholars.

Liberation theologians read the text, attending primarily to what they perceive are the needs of their contemporary society, doing so in the light of the modern political philosophy of Marxism.[60] Such a reading will bring certain elements of the text into prominence, in particular, those texts concerning the liberation of the oppressed. The Exodus, which is certainly a major biblical theme, takes on even larger proportions in the writings of theologians of liberation.

There are many differences among biblical scholars who operate under the rubric of feminism.[61] Some wish simply to explore the characters, books, and themes that are relevant to the situation of the modern woman. Studies of female characters, such as the wives of David, are an example. Others want to read the whole text from a female perspective to see what difference it makes for the implied reader to be a woman. Still others wish to read the Bible as women in order to "explode the

---

[59] A. Thiselton, *The Two Horizons: New Testament Hermeneutics and Philosophical Description* (Grand Rapids: Eerdmans, 1980).

[60] I include here not only those scholars who *recognize* that they are reader-response critics but some who would assert that they are text oriented (e.g., N. Gottwald, *The Tribes of Yahweh* [Maryknoll: Orbis, 1979]).

[61] See the collected studies and bibliographies in *JSOT* 22 (1982).

myth of patriarchy"—that is, to show the innate prejudice of
the Scriptures against women and to expose the Bible as a tool
of oppression. They are united in the sense that they approach
the text with an agenda. Many utilize reader-response theory
for their theoretical justification.

While extreme forms of liberation theology and feminism
must be rejected and caution must be taken regarding all forms
of ideological reading on the grounds that distortion is possible
or even likely, much may nevertheless be learned from these
perspectives. These readers bring out themes of Scripture that
are commonly passed over by most readers of the Bible—
concern for the poor, the role of women, and so forth.

We must remember that *no one* can approach the biblical
text objectively or with a completely open mind. Indeed, such
an approach to the text would be undesirable. Everyone comes
to the text with questions and an agenda. One's attitude,
however, should be one of openness toward change.

Consideration of the need for openness leads to a brief
comment on contextualization.[62] Evangelical theologians and
biblical scholars are becoming increasingly sensitive to the fact
that each reader approaches the Scriptures with certain cultural
and personal questions and assumptions.[63] We are not neutral
and objective as we approach the text. We come at it from
different perspectives. This preunderstanding will influence our
interpretation of Scripture. The issue is not one of incorrect
interpretation but of our giving prominence to certain parts of
the text and not to others. We might read, say, the Song of
Songs as a single man or woman and then some time later as a
young married person and find that our attention is drawn to
different aspects of the text.

Christian thinkers recognize this phenomenon as existing
also between cultures. A Christian from Egypt, one from the
United States, and one from China will each come to the text
with different questions and needs. The Scriptures are the same

---

[62] See H. Conn, *Eternal Word and Changing Worlds* (Grand Rapids: Zondervan, 1984).

[63] See Thiselton, *The Two Horizons*.

for each. The preunderstanding of the interpreter encounters the text and *must* conform to it. Contextualization implies not that the interpreter creates meaning but simply that the interpretation of the biblical text involves its application to the respective contemporary situations.

DECONSTRUCTION

Literary Studies

The cutting edge of literary studies in the mid-1980s is deconstruction.[64] It is the "new wave" from France. Like the previous imports (existentialism, structuralism), deconstruction has brought strong reactions, both positive and negative, from English and American scholars.

I discuss deconstruction at the end of this survey of literary theory, not simply because it is the most prominent of recent approaches. Each of the other theories emphasizes one of the elements of the act of literary communication: author, text, or reader. Deconstruction, on the contrary, questions the grounds of all these approaches. Culler, in his insightful analysis comments, "It demonstrates the difficulties of any theory that would define meaning in a univocal way: as what an author intends, what conventions determine, what a reader experiences."[65] Deconstruction, therefore, stands outside of the pattern of the other theories and is treated separately.

As with New Criticism and structuralism, it must be said that deconstruction is "[not a] method, system, or settled body of ideas."[66] This caveat takes on special force since, as will be seen below, deconstruction is constantly in danger of taking itself too seriously and thus becoming another text-centered theory.

---

[64] There are already indications, however, that the deconstruction school is no longer avant-garde. D. Tracy, *Plurality and Ambiguity* (San Francisco: Harper and Row, 1987), is a post-deconstructionist statement in hermeneutics.

[65] J. Culler, *On Deconstruction: Theory and Criticism After Structuralism* (London: Routledge & Kegan Paul, 1982), p. 131.

[66] C. Norris, *Deconstruction: Theory and Practice* (London: Methuen, 1982), p. 1.

Deconstruction is most closely associated with Jacques Derrida. His first major writings appeared in 1967, but his major influence came in the 1970s and continues in the 1980s. Derrida is part philosopher and part literary critic, but his impact has occurred in the latter field, though in his hands the division between these two disciplines becomes quite fluid. Derrida, indeed, attacks the Western philosophical tradition that subordinates writing to speaking. Since at least Plato, speech has been thought to bear a closer relationship to pure thought than does writing. Writing removes communication a step further from authorial presence. Derrida argues that this attitude, which underlies Western philosophy, demonstrates a stubborn belief in *presence*. Ultimately, such a belief is grounded in what he calls "a transcendental signified," which Abrams describes as "an absolute foundation, outside the play of language itself, which is adequate to 'center' (that is, to anchor and organize) the linguistic system in such a way as to fix the particular meaning of a spoken or written discourse within that system."[67]

Derrida argues instead for the priority of writing over speech. He believes that writing is a clearer illustration of what characterizes all language acts: the slippage between sign and referent, signifier and signified. Derrida's extreme language skepticism calls into question the act of literary communication. Characteristic of Derrida is an analysis of pivotal philosophers such as Plato, Rousseau, Saussure, Lévi-Strauss, and Austin. He exposes their *logocentricism* (belief in a "metaphysics of presence"), which is implied in their fundamental *phonocentricism* (priority of speech over writing). He probes the text of these philosophers until he uncovers an *aporia* (a basic contradiction), which usually involves the philosopher's use of metaphor or some other rhetorical device. Metaphor is key in this regard because it displays the slippage between sign and referent. Its use by the philosopher demonstrates, contra the philosophers, that the truth claims of philosophy are no different from those of fiction.

---

[67] Abrams, *Glossary*, p. 38.

The fundamental force behind Derrida's writing is his heightening the distance between signifier and signified. Here he threatens the possibility of literary communication. He begins with Saussure's premise that a sign has no inherent meaning but finds meaning only in distinction to other elements in the semiotic system. Meaning is thus a function not of presence but of absence. Derrida's concept of *différance* is helpful here. (The *a* in *différance* shows that the word is a neologism, constructed from two different French words, one meaning " to differ," the other "to defer.") The meaning of a linguistic or literary sign is based on its difference in comparison with other signs and as such is always deferred, or delayed. With deconstruction one enters the "endless labyrinth."[68] Meaning is never established; the pun becomes the favored interpretive device.

The main bastion of American deconstruction has been at Yale. G. Hartman, H. Bloom, P. DeMan, and J. Hillis Miller, though different from Derrida and from each other, have been identified as his most able representatives.[69] Some advocates for deconstruction have expressed fear that deconstruction may be threatened by its routine use in the study of texts. They fear that some scholars are applying Derrida's style of analysis to texts mechanically, which may signal its demise.

At present, however, deconstruction is alive and well and is threatened seriously only by Marxist or political interpreters. Marxist interpreters disdain deconstruction, since it removes literature and the critic from any meaningful interaction with the world. Derrida's motto "there is nothing outside of the text" irritates them. The clash between this-worldly and no-worldly interpretation will continue into the next decade.

Michael Edwards provides brief, but tantalizing, comments on deconstruction from a Christian perspective.[70] Instead of criticizing Derrida, he points out the fundamental insight into

---

[68] Lentricchia, *After the New Criticism,* p. 166.

[69] See V. B. Leitch, *Deconstructive Criticism: An Advanced Introduction* (New York: Columbia University Press, 1983), and more popularly, Campbell, "Tyranny."

[70] M. Edwards, *Towards a Christian Poetics* (London: Macmillan, 1984).

the nature of language that Derrida provides. Edwards does not gainsay Derrida's fundamental atheism but points out that like most non-Christian philosophers, Derrida builds on an essentially true insight. Edwards claims that Derrida is right to point out the extreme difficulties in communication. There are fissures or breaks between words and their referents. Derrida attributes this slippage to an absence of the "transcendental signified" (i.e., God), Edwards to the Fall.

Biblical Studies

Presently there are few signs of Derridean influence on biblical studies. We have observed, however, that every major school of thought has eventually influenced biblical studies, and there is no reason to doubt that deconstruction will follow suit.

To say that no influence has been registered would be incorrect. *Semeia* 23 (1982) is entitled *Derrida and Biblical Studies*. Furthermore, the New Testament scholar John Dominic Crossan has been active in bringing Derrida's thought to bear on issues of interpretation. This influence is most readily seen in his book *Cliffs of Fall: Paradox and Polyvalence in the Parables of Jesus* (1980), in which he analyzes the parables from a Derridean perspective. He finds that the metaphoricity of the parable has a "void of meaning at its core. . . . it can mean so many things and generate so many differing interpretations because it has no fixed, univocal or absolute meaning to begin with."[71] Instead of searching for the meaning of the parable, he *plays* (a favorite metaphor of deconstructive method) with the words of the text.

Perhaps the most explicit deconstructive study of Old Testament texts is found in Peter Miscall's *The Workings of Old Testament Narrative*. He devotes the bulk of his book to a close reading of Genesis 12 and 1 Samuel 16–22. For Miscall, such a reading reveals information that is insufficient for arriving at a single meaning. "There is, at the same time, too little and too much of the narrative, too few and too many details, and this

---

[71] J. D. Crossan, *Cliffs of Falls* (New York: Seabury, 1980), pp. 9–10; see also G. Aichele, Jr., *The Limits of Story* (Philadelphia: Fortress, 1985).

gives rise to the many, and frequently contradictory, interpretations of and conjectures about OT narrative."[72] He concludes that to attempt to pin down a single meaning of the text is misguided and argues that most exegetical issues are undecidable: "The reading encounters ambiguity, equivocation, opposed meanings and cannot decide for or establish one or the other; the reading cannot stop, it cannot control or limit the text."[73]

In his analysis of the David and Goliath story, for example, Miscall concentrates on both the concrete details of the text as well as the gaps, for instance, information not given in the text about a character's motivation. By such an analysis of the text of 1 Samuel 17, Miscall claims that

> David's character is undecidable. The text permits us to regard David as a pious and innocent young shepherd going to battle the Philistine because of the latter's defiance of the Lord and as a cunning and ambitious young warrior who is aware of the effects that his defeat of Goliath will have on the assembled army.[74]

In the postscript Miscall explicitly connects his readings with a deconstructive approach to the text. He points out instances he finds of aporia, of inherent contradictions in the text. He argues that the type of ambiguity he thus demonstrates is the result of the nature of literary communication (the slippage of signifier and signified) and that the Bible, like other works of literature, always deconstructs itself.

---

[72] P. D. Miscall, *The Workings of Old Testament Narrative* (Philadelphia Fortress, 1983), p. 1.

[73] Ibid., p. 2.

[74] Ibid., p. 73.

2

AN APPRAISAL OF THE LITERARY APPROACH

Having reviewed the history of the literary study of the Bible, we may now proceed to evaluation.[1] What are the disadvantages or even dangers of a literary approach, and can they be avoided? Are there benefits to be gained by analyzing the biblical text from this perspective?

PITFALLS

The Different Literary Approaches Are Contradictory

The first difficulty with the literary approach is that the field of secular literary theory and the related discipline of linguistics are divided among themselves. There is much infighting about the basic questions of literature and interpretation as a number of different schools of thought seek domination in the field. The biblical scholar faces a dilemma at this point. Students of the Bible find it difficult enough to keep abreast of their own field without keeping current with a second one. The usual result is that biblical scholars follow one particular school of thought or else one particularly prominent

---

[1] This chapter was published in an earlier form as "The Literary Approach to the Study of the Old Testament: Pitfalls and Promise," *JETS* 28 (1985): 385–98.

thinker as their guide to a literary approach. Because of the natural desire to seem current or avant-garde, the most current theory is commonly adopted.

Francis Schaeffer described the lag that occurs between biblical studies and the rest of the disciplines.[2] A new philosophical approach that comes on the scene influences art, literary theory, sociology, music, and then finally biblical studies. This process may be observed in the case of Derrida's deconstruction. It gained prominence in the late 1960s and early 1970s and just now is making an impact on biblical studies.

My concern is that the hard-and-fast school divisions in literary theory are imported into biblical studies with little methodological reflection. Every major movement in literary theory of the past forty years is mirrored in the work of biblical scholars: New Criticism (Weiss, Childs); Northrup Frye's archetypal approach to literature (Frye himself, Ryken); phenomenology (Detweiler, Ricoeur); structuralist (Jobling, Polzin, Patte); Marxism (Gottwald, liberation theologians); feminism (Trible, Reuther, Fiorenza); deconstruction (Crossan, Miscall).

The apologist must analyze the deep philosophical roots of each of these schools of thought. Students of the Bible and biblical scholars working on method, however, can recognize positive, though perhaps distorted, insights that each of these schools provides. I thus agree with John Barton, who has said that "all of the methods . . . have something in them, but none of them is the 'correct method.'" In his view, our methods are best seen as "codification of intuitions about the text which may occur to intelligent readers."[3]

Among the many positive contributions that may be gleaned from each of these schools of thought we could include the New Critical insight that we must focus our interpretation on the text rather than on the author's background; the structuralist attention to literary conventions; and the emphasis

---

[2] F. A. Schaeffer, *The God Who Is There* (Downers Grove, Ill.: InterVarsity, 1968), pp. 13–84.

[3] Barton, *Reading the Old Testament*, p. 5.

of feminism and Marxism on the themes of sexual and economic justice. Even deconstruction may give us an insight into the effect of the Fall on language, namely, the schism between signifier and signified.[4]

Notice that in each case the secular theory leads to a new imbalance. New Criticism rightly attacked certain cases of appealing to the author's intention for the meaning of a text, but it went too far in restricting the interpreter to the text alone, the text as artifact, leaving both author and reader out of the picture. Marxist and feminist readings distort the text by insisting that their themes are the only interpretive grids. And deconstructionists use their insight into the slippage between sign and object to attack theology or any type of literary communication.

The literary approach thus easily and often falls into the application of one particular (and usually current) literary theory to the biblical text. Biblical scholars, however, except in a very few exceptional cases, are not experts in a second field and therefore fall prey to the current theoretical fashion. The best approach in such a situation is an eclectic one. The Christian interpreter must reject any methodological insights that fundamentally conflict with basic Christian convictions but can, because of common grace, glean helpful insights from all fields of scholarship.

Literary Theory Is Often Obscurantist

The second pitfall is related to the first: literary theory is often obscurantist. Each school of thought develops its own in-language. Actant, *signifié,* narratology, interpretant, *différance,* and aporia are only a few among the many esoteric terms of the field. An illustration of the type of obscurantism to which I am referring is found in the structuralist analysis of the Book of Job by Robert Polzin. Following the method of the famous anthropologist Claude Lévi-Strauss, Polzin summarizes the

---

[4] Edwards, *Towards a Christian Perspective,* pp. 217–37.

message of the Book of Job with the following math-like formula:[5]

$$F_x(a):F_y(b) \cong F_x(b):F_{a-1}(y)$$

While we need not argue against technical terminology, neither must we glory in it. When new technical terms are introduced into scholarly discussion, they must be carefully defined, a precaution that most theoretical discussions seem to ignore.

The solution is not to throw out the literary approach but rather to seek clarity of expression. It is interesting that the two books that have had the biggest impact on biblical scholarship in the area of literary approach are Robert Alter's *The Art of Biblical Narrative* and James Kugel's *The Idea of Biblical Poetry*. Each one uses little technical jargon and gives much straightforward help in the explication of texts.

The Theory May Impose Western Concepts on Ancient Literature

The next danger is that of imposing modern Western concepts and categories on an ancient Semitic literature. If done, according to some critics of the literary approach, it could lead to a radical distortion of the text. On the surface of it, the danger appears real. Modern literary theory develops its concepts from its encounter with modern literature. Propp and Greimas developed their theories of the structure of folk tales by analyzing Russian stories.[6] This schema has been applied to biblical stories by many, notably Roland Barthes.[7] Theories of Hebrew metrics are usually based on systems employed in other modern poetic traditions. The oral basis of much of biblical literature is supposedly uncovered by means of comparisons with classical and Yugoslavian oral literature.[8]

---

[5] Polzin, *Biblical Structuralism*, p. 75.

[6] Propp, *Morphology of the Folktale* and Greimas, *Structural Semantics*.

[7] R. Barthes, "La lutte avec l'ange: Analyse textuelle de Genèse 32.23–33," in *Analyse structurale et exégèse biblique*, pp. 27–40.

[8] F. M. Cross, "Prose and Poetry in the Mythic and Epic Texts from Ugarit," *HTR* 67 (1974): 1–15; see A. B. Lord, *The Singer of Tales* (Cambridge: Harvard University Press, 1964).

Such a list could be lengthened considerably and apparently manifests an insensitivity toward what Anthony Thiselton calls the two horizons of the act of interpretation.[9] The ancient text comes from a culture far removed in time and space from that of the modern interpreter. This distance must be taken into account in our interpretation or else the exegesis will be distorted by reading modern values and presuppositions into the ancient text.

James Kugel is the harshest critic of the literary method from this perspective. He expresses his reservations theoretically in an article entitled "On the Bible and Literary Criticism" and practically in his justly acclaimed *Idea of Biblical Poetry*.[10] In the latter work he points out that biblical Hebrew has no word for "poetry." Thus, Kugel comments, "to speak of 'poetry' at all in the Bible will be in some measure to impose a concept foreign to the biblical world."[11] He also rightly points out that no single characteristic or group of characteristics can differentiate prose from poetry in the Hebrew Bible. Parallelism in fact occurs also in prose, and poetic meter does not exist. Instead of using the designation *poetry* to describe a distinct genre in the Old Testament, Kugel prefers to speak of "high style."

While one may agree with Kugel to a large extent, Kugel goes too far in rejecting the generic term *poetry*. If one reads a psalm and then a chapter of Numbers, one immediately notices a difference. On one level we can contrast the short, terse lines of the psalm with the lengthy lines of Numbers. There is also a heightening of certain rhetorical devices in the psalm that normally would not be found in the same magnitude in the Numbers section. In the psalm we encounter parallelism, metaphors, less restriction on the syntax, and so forth. In this relatively greater terseness and heightened use of rhetorical devices, we see a literary phenomenon that is related to our own distinction between poetry and prose. Kugel of course recognizes most of these differences but still hesitates to name the

[9] Thiselton, *The Two Horizons*.

[10] J. Kugel, "On the Bible and Literary Criticism," *Prooftexts* 1 (1981): 99–104; idem, *The Idea of Biblical Poetry*.

[11] Kugel, *The Idea of Biblical Poetry*, p. 69.

psalm poetic. His hesitation stems from the fear of distorting biblical materials by imposing foreign literary constructs on them.

On another level, not discussed by Kugel, the two passages differ in their relative deviance from common speech. Numbers is closer to common speech patterns than the psalms passage. In any literary tradition, poetry is characterized by its being further removed from common, everyday speech than is prose. The difference between prose and poetry is relative, and we must not downplay the obvious literary artifice in the prose sections of Scripture. But the difference is substantial enough to be called a generic distinction, and our modern categories of prose and poetry are the closest to the phenomenon we discover in the Bible.

I have struggled with this issue, particularly in the area of genre theory, as I worked on fifteen Akkadian texts that I described as fictional autobiographies. Since many would not date the beginning of autobiography until Rousseau in the eighteenth century, I needed to justify my genre iden-tification.[12] We know that there is not universal generic similarity. New genres develop; old ones die out.[13] In addition, certain cultures use some genres and neglect others. For example, in the ancient world there is nothing comparable to the modern novel. In the same way, twentieth-century Ameri-can literature contains few if any omens. Nevertheless, though a culture-free genre system does not exist, the native literary classification of each culture (or lack of such classification, as in the case of the distinction between prose and poetry in Hebrew) need not be adopted uncritically in order to identify the genres of that culture.

The separation of etic and emic approaches to literature deals with these cultural determinants in literary classification.[14]

---

[12] T. Longman III, *Fictional Akkadian Autobiography* (Winona Lake, Ind.: Eisenbrauns, forthcoming).

[13] A. Fowler, "The Life and Death of Literary Forms," *New Literary History* 2 (1970–71): 199–216.

[14] K. Pike, *Language in Relation to a Unified Theory of Human Behavior* (The Hague: Mouton, 1967), chap. 2; and V. S. Poythress, "Analysing a Biblical

The emic describes native designations and classification of literature. This approach has the advantage of giving the researcher insight into the native consciousness of a particular text and also the relationship between that text and others bearing the same designation. The etic view of literature imposes a nonnative grid or classification scheme not necessarily defined in their language. While there is always the danger of distorting understanding of the texts by imposing foreign standards on them, it must be pointed out that Israelite scribes were not concerned with a precise and self-conscious generic classification of their literature. Both were innovations of the Greeks. While the biblical authors identified song (*šîr*), proverb (*māšāl*) and other speech forms, which provide helpful keys to research, they are predictably not systematic or rigorous in their categorization.

Secular Theory Eliminates the Author

The next pitfall is the danger of moving completely away from any concept of authorial intent and determinant meaning of a text. As we noted in chapter 1, secular theory since the advent of New Criticism in the middle of this century has united in its denial of any significance for the author. Traditional criticism before that point displayed considerable interest in the author and his or her background. The emphasis now has been redirected. Literature is an act of communication that may be described as a dynamic between poet, poem, and audience, or between author, text, and reader. Attention has been drawn by New Criticism and structuralism primarily to the text, and by reader-response theories (including those of Iser and Fish,

---

Text: Some Important Linguistic Distinctions," *SJT* 32 (1979): 113–37. The emic/etic distinction was first proposed in linguistics, where it was used to distinguish native understanding of language from the analysis of a language by linguists or other outsiders. Pike was the first to generalize the distinction into a principle that could be used in the study of any aspect of culture. Poythress further refined the concept. For the tendency of taking linguistic categories and applying them to other disciplines, see J. Culler, *The Pursuit of Signs* (Ithaca: Cornell University Press, 1981), pp. 27–29.

feminism, and Marxism) to the reader and the reader's constitutive participation in the formation of meaning in the literary act.

One major voice has dissented from this trend. E. D. Hirsch posits an author-centered interpretive method that seeks to arrive at the author's intent.[15] This approach, Hirsch believes, provides an anchor of determinant meaning in the sea of relativity introduced by other theories. Although Hirsch's views have not been widely accepted by his fellow literary theorists, his emphasis provides a needed counterbalance to the trends in secular theory.

I comment further on this fourth pitfall when I discuss below the promises of the literary approach. Somewhat paradoxically, while there is danger in moving away from authorial intent, there is also benefit in the fact that the literary approach focuses our attention more on the text than on the author during the act of interpretation.

Contemporary Theory Denies Referential Function to Literature

The last pitfall is the most significant. Along with the move away from the author in contemporary theory, one can also note the tendency to deny or to limit severely any referential function to literature. "The poet affirmeth nothing," states Philip Sidney. Frank Lentricchia's masterful *After the New Criticism* follows the history of literary theory for the last forty years, using the theme of the denial of any external reference for literature. Literature in this view represents not an insight into the world but rather a limitless semiotic play.

Perhaps this modern tendency goes back to Saussure's theory of the sign. In his view, there is no natural connection between the signifier and the signified. The relationship between the two is arbitrary, or conventional. For Saussure, the fact that different languages have different words for the horse, for example, indicates that the relationship is arbitrary and determined by custom. Also note that, according to Saussure

---

[15] See chapter 1, "Author-centered Theories."

and the semiotic tradition that emanates from his writings, the sign does not point to an object in reality. The sign unites an acoustical image with a concept, rather than a word with a thing.[16] (The word sign might point to a nonexistent or metaphorical horse.)

In any case the rupture between the literary and the referential is an axiom of modern literary theory. As one might expect, recognition of the literary characteristics of the Bible has led scholars to equate the Bible and literature, with the corollary that the Bible as a literary text does not refer outside of itself and, in particular, makes no reference to history. This position leads on the part of some to a complete or substantial denial of a historical approach to the text, which most often takes the form of denying or denigrating traditional historical–critical methods. Source and form criticism particularly are attacked. The following quotations represent the views of some who adopt the literary approach.

> Above all, we must keep in mind that narrative is a *form of representation*. Abraham in Genesis is not a real person any more than the painting of an apple is real fruit.

> Once the unity of the story is experienced, one is able to participate in the world of the story. Although the author of the Gospel of Mark certainly used sources rooted in the historical events surrounding the life of Jesus, the final text is a literary creation with an autonomous integrity, just as Leonardo's portrait of the Mona Lisa exists independently as a vision of life apart from any resemblance or nonresemblance to the person who posed for it or as a play of Shakespeare has integrity apart from reference to the historical characters depicted there. Thus, Mark's narrative contains a closed and self-sufficient world with its own integrity. . . . When viewed as a literary achievement the statements in Mark's narrative, rather than being a representation of historical events, refer to the people, places, and events *in the story*.

> As long as readers require the gospel to be a window to the ministry of Jesus before they will see truth in it, accepting the gospel will mean believing that the story it tells corresponds

---

[16] F. Lentricchia, *After the New Criticism*, p. 118.

exactly to what actually happened during Jesus' ministry. When the gospel is viewed as a mirror, though of course not a mirror in which we see only ourselves, its meaning can be found on this side of it, that is, between text and reader, in the experience of reading the text, and belief in the gospel can mean openness to the ways it calls readers to interact with it, with life, and with their own world. . . . The real issue is whether "his story" can be true if it is not history.[17]

For these authors, the truth of "his story" is independent of any historical information.

Similar evaluation may be seen in the hermeneutics of Hans Frei, who pinpoints the major error in both traditional critical and conservative exegesis in the loss of the understanding that biblical narrative is history-like and not true history with an ostensive, or external, reference.[18] Alter's brilliant analysis of Old Testament narrative is coupled with the assumption that the nature of the narrative is "historicized fiction," or fictional history.[19]

The result of this approach is a turning away from historical investigation of the text as impossible or irrelevant. The traditional methods of historical criticism are abandoned or radically modified or given secondary consideration. Concern to discover the original *Sitz im Leben* or to discuss the tradition history of a text languishes among this new breed of scholar. This attitude understandably concerns traditional critical scholarship, so that we find among recent articles ones like Leander Keck's "Will the Historical-Critical Method Survive?"[20] While evangelicals might in some respects be glad to see the end of

---

[17] Berlin, *Poetics and Interpretation*, p. 13; D. Rhoads and D. Michie, *Mark as Story: The Introduction to the Narrative of a Gospel* (Philadelphia: Fortress, 1982), pp. 3–4; R. A. Culpepper, *Anatomy of the Fourth Gospel* (Philadelphia: Fortress, 1983), pp. 236–37.

[18] H. Frei, *The Eclipse of Biblical Narrative* (New Haven: Yale University Press, 1974).

[19] Alter, *The Art of Biblical Narrative*.

[20] Leander Keck, "Will the Historical-Critical Method Survive?" in *Orientation by Disorientation*, ed. R. A. Spencer (Pittsburgh: Pickwick, 1980), pp. 115–27.

historical criticism, they, along with historical critics, have a high stake in the question of history.

According to Wellek and Warren in their *Theory of Literature,* the distinguishing characteristics of literature are fictionality, invention, and imagination. To identify Genesis simply as a work of literature is thus to move it out of the realm of history. This characterizes some, if not much, of the literary approach to the study of the Old Testament.

Frye's comment, quoted above in the introduction, suggests an alternative approach: "The Bible is as literary as it can well be without actually being literature."[21] We thus may consider Genesis, for example, more than simply literature. On the one hand, Genesis is not reducible to a work of fiction. On the other hand, we must apply a literary approach because it possesses literary qualities.

Another distinguishing characteristic of literature is its self-conscious structure and expression. In Russian formalist terms, language is *foregrounded.* As the framework hypothesis has pointed out, there is literary artifice in the parallelism between the first three days of creation and the last three.[22] Similarly, literary craft is displayed in the symmetrical structures of the Flood story, in the Babel story, or moving beyond Genesis, in the Solomon narrative.[23]

The point is that we do not have so-called objective, neutral, or unshaped reporting of events. (As many have pointed out, there is no such thing as a brute fact; an uninterpreted historical report is inconceivable.) Genesis is clearly not attempting to report events dispassionately. Rather it contains proclamation, which shapes the history to differing degrees. The biblical narrators are concerned not only to tell us facts but also to guide our perspective and responses to those events.

---

[21] Frye, *The Great Code,* p. 62.

[22] See among others, M. G. Kline, "Because It Had Not Rained," *WTJ* 20 (1958): 146–57.

[23] Wenham, "The Coherence"; J. P. Fokkelmann, *Narrative Art in Genesis* (Assen: van Gorcum, 1975), pp. 11ff.; R. B. Dillard, "The Literary Structure of the Chronicler's Solomon Narrative," *JSOT* 30 (1984): 85–93.

Old Testament prose narrative may thus be described as selective, structured, emphasized, and interpreted stories. The author/narrator controls the way in which we view the events. Here we can see how plot analysis, narrator studies, character studies, point-of-view analysis, and suspense-creating devices may be helpful, though definitely partial, approaches toward the understanding of a text.

The question of historical truth boils down to the question of who ultimately is guiding us in our interpretation of these events. If we look ultimately to human authors, then literary art may be deceptive. If we look to God, then we cannot have deception. A literary analysis of a historical book is thus not incompatible with a high view of the historicity of the text, including the view that affirms the inerrancy and infallibility of Scripture in the area of history. (I do not want to give the mistaken impression that all of Scripture is historical in nature. The generic intention of each book and each section needs to be analyzed before attributing a historical reference to the book.)

We should note that some scholars argue that literature is an act of communication between the writer and the reader, an act that functions in more than one way. Besides a poetic function, the text may also have a referential function, according to Roman Jakobson's communication model of literary discourse.[24] Of course, the poetic function may become so dominant that the referential function ceases to exist, so that truly "the poet affirmeth nothing." The opposite pole is reached when there is a concerted effort to rid the text of self-referential language (i.e., metaphor), an impossible goal, as it is in scientific discourse. The biblical text for the most part is somewhere in between.

PROMISES

While there are potential pitfalls in pursuing a literary approach to biblical interpretation, we see that they are

---

[24] Cf. N. R. Petersen, *Literary Criticism for New Testament Critics* (Philadelphia: Fortress, 1978), pp. 33ff.

avoidable. Positively, though, what value is there in a literary approach? I have hinted at answers a number of times: while not to be reduced to literature pure and simple, the Bible is nonetheless amenable to literary analysis. Indeed, some of the most illuminating work done on the Bible in the past decade has been from a literary point of view, often done by literary scholars. Biblical scholars, particularly traditional critics, do not always make the most sensitive readers as C. S. Lewis once complained:

> Whatever these men may be as Biblical critics, I distrust them as critics. They seem to me to lack literary judgment, to be imperceptive about the very quality of the texts they are reading. . . . These men ask me to believe they can read between the lines of the old texts; the evidence is their obvious inability to read (in any sense worth discussing) the lines themselves. They claim to see fern-seed and can't see an elephant ten yards away in broad daylight.[25]

A literary approach, however, offers promise in three general areas.

Literary Theory Reveals the Conventions of Biblical Literature

A literary approach assists us in understanding the conventions of biblical storytelling. Alter has observed that

> every culture, even every era in a particular culture, develops distinctive and sometimes intricate codes for telling its stories, involving everything from narrative point of view, procedures of description and characterization, the management of dialogue, to the ordering of time and the organization of plot.[26]

The literary text is an act of communication from writer to reader. The text is the message. For it to communicate, the sender and receiver have to speak the same language. The writer, through the use of conventional forms, sends signals to

---

[25] C. S. Lewis, *Fern-seed and Elephants* (Glasgow: Collins, 1975), pp. 106, 111.
[26] R. Alter, "A Response to Critics," *JSOT* 27 (1983): 113–17.

the readers to tell them how they are to take the message. We all know the generic signals in English (e.g., "once upon a time," "a novel by . . ."); we recognize poetry by all the white spaces on the page.

A literary approach explores and makes explicit the conventions of biblical literature in order to understand the message it intends to carry. It is significant to discover that Deuteronomy is in the form of a treaty, that the narrator shapes the reader's response to the characters of a text in different ways, and that repetition is not necessarily a sign of multiple sources but a literary device.

Now in ordinary reading we recognize much of this information automatically. We passively let the narrator shape our interpretation of the event being reported to us, we make an unconscious genre identification, and so forth. As interpreters of a text, however, it is important to make these conventions explicit, even more so with the Bible, since it is an ancient text and the conventions employed are often not ones we are used to.

A Literary Approach Stresses Whole Texts

Evangelicals commonly tend to atomize the text and to focus attention on a word or a few verses. Traditional critical scholarship displays the same tendency for a different reason, not believing that the whole text is original. The literary approach asks the question of the force of the whole. For this reason many evangelical scholars have seen the literary approach serving an apologetic function. If it can be shown that the Joseph narrative, the Flood narrative, the rise of the monarchy section (1 Sam. 8–12), and the Book of Judges are all examples of literary wholes, then we apparently have little use for source criticism.[27]

---

[27] Wenham, "The Coherence"; L. Eslinger, "Viewpoints and Point of View in I Samuel 8–12," *JSOT* 26 (1983): 61–76; D. W. Gooding, "The Composition of the Book of Judges," *EI* 16 (1982): 70–79.

Literary Theory Focuses on the Reading Process

Work in literary criticism helps us to understand the reading process. I described above the act of literary communication as the author sending a message (text) to the reader. In the act of interpretation our focus must be on the text. As Geoffrey Strickland has said, "All that we say or think about a particular utterance or piece of writing presupposes an assumption on our part, correct or otherwise, concerning the intention of the speaker or writer."[28] But we must also recognize the role of readers and their predisposition as they approach the text. While not advocating the view of some reader-response theorists that readers actually create the meaning of the text— rather, the text imposes restrictions on possible interpretations—we must recognize that the readers' background and their interests will lead them to attend to certain parts of the Bible's message more than other parts.

In this connection we must consider the relevance of contextualization and multiperspectival approaches to the text. We also must mention here the value of what might be called ideological readers, even when they are unbalanced. Feminists and liberation theologians, for example, read the Bible with colored glasses, which often leads to distortion, but such readers do bring out important issues and themes that other, less interested, readers miss. My basic point here is that reading involves the interaction of the writer with the reader through the text, so that any theory that concentrates on one of the three to the exclusion of the others may be distorted.[29]

More could be said about the promise and benefits of a literary approach. In the final analysis, however, the proof is the illuminating exegesis that this approach has led to. I refer to such insightful analyses as those of R. Alter, C. Conroy, A.

---

[28] G. Strickland, *Structuralism or Criticism? Thoughts on How We Read* (Cambridge: Cambridge University Press, 1981), p. 36.

[29] After completing this chapter, I had occasion to read the helpful introductory book by L. Ryken, *Windows to the World* (Grand Rapids: Zondervan, 1985), which also adopts what I consider to be a balanced view of the dynamics of reading.

Berlin, R. A. Culpepper, D. Gunn, and others listed in the section on further reading at the end of the book. Following a review of basic principles in chapter 3, I turn in part 2 to a discussion of several specific examples.

3

BASIC PRINCIPLES

Thus far we have surveyed the history of literary approaches to the study of the Bible and have analyzed their positive and negative features. Along the way we have pointed to a positive program for literary readings of biblical texts. Before applying literary insights to particular prose and poetry texts, however, it will be advantageous to summarize and explicate more fully some of the major theoretical premises upon which the studies in part 2 are based. I consider, then, the act of literary communication and several functions of biblical literature.

THE ACT OF LITERARY COMMUNICATION

Communication involves a message that a sender directs toward a receiver. Different media may be used to send a message. A message may be (1) oral in face-to-face conversation, a phone call, or a radio show; (2) sent by signals of one sort or another; or (3) written. Literature is a subset of this third type of communication between a sender and receiver.

In the act of literary communication, the sender may be referred to as the author or the poet. The message is the text or literary work, and the receiver is the reader, the critic, or the audience. We have already observed that the various schools of thought concerning the interpretation of literary texts may be distinguished on the basis of which aspect of the act of literary communication (if any) they emphasize. Traditional interpretation emphasizes the author and his or her background; New Criticism and structuralism focus on the text; reader-response theory concentrates on the reader; and deconstruction questions the very idea of communication through literature.

While it is dangerous to generalize, we could suggest that this proliferation of approaches is the result of loss of faith in the act of literary communication. Since it is impossible to be absolutely certain and completely exhaustive about the meaning of a particular text, scholars have often abandoned the notion of determinant meaning in literature.

Such a loss of faith is unnecessary if we realize that our interpretations of any text, and biblical literature in particular, are partial, hypothetical, probable, and contextualized. Said positively, our interpretations may never be dogmatic, because the texts are rich in meaning, the mind of God (the final author) is ultimately unfathomable, and, recognizing that interpretation necessarily includes application, the situations that readers confront are various.

Many of our interpretations will be highly probable to the point of being nearly certain, but we must always retain a certain level of humility in our interpretations because of our inability to read the mind of the author of a text. Such an understanding of the interpretive process not only allows us to regain faith in the interpretive process but permits us to understand why there are legitimate differences of interpretation between readers. The position advocated in this book is that the biblical authors communicated to readers through texts. By way of summary and explication, I briefly review each of the elements of the communicative process.

Author

If literature is an act of communication, then meaning resides in the intention of the author. The author has encoded a message for the readers. Interpretation then has as its goal the recovery of the author's purpose in writing. The difficulties involved in such a position have been recognized in chapter 2. The hypothetical and probable nature of interpretation enters the picture because we cannot read minds and thus cannot be absolutely certain that we have recovered the correct meaning of a text. This fact should not lead us to throw up our hands in despair. As the next section indicates, there are constraints imposed on the meaning that an interpreter may impute to the author. The view that the author is the locus of the meaning of a text provides theoretical stability to interpretation. Our interpretation is correct insofar as it conforms to the meaning intended by the author.

When speaking of the author in the Bible, a number of questions arise that cannot be fully discussed here. One issue involves the composition of various books of the Bible and the issue of the use of sources and the levels of redaction. Here I use "author" to refer most pointedly to the final shaper of a canonical book. When I read Chronicles, I am interested in the intention of the author/redactor of that book and not in the intention of the author/redactor of his sources (say, the canonical Deuteronomic History). In other words, I am interested in how and for what purpose the final author uses his source.

A second issue concerning the intention of the author is the relationship between the human author and the divine author. God is the ultimate author of the Scriptures, so it must be said that final meaning resides in His intention. Of course, He condescended to reveal His message to the biblical authors, who did not write in a trance but had conscious intentions of their own. But it is wrong to equate fully the intention of God with that of the human author. For instance, the application in the New Testament of an Old Testament text frequently exceeds the obvious meaning intended by the author of the latter.[1]

---

[1] Kaiser, *Toward an Exegetical Theology,* pp. 108–14, in his legitimate concern to restrain eisegetical tendencies inherent in *sensus plenior* and other readings that appeal to God's ultimate authorship, swings the pendulum too far in the other direction by denying that there is any difference between the human and divine

Before going on to the next closely related topic, I mention the importance of background studies. The study of the historical context of an author is helpful, since it places constraints on interpretation and helps to elucidate the meaning of a text. About the author Nahum, for example, we know only that he came from Elkosh, a town that we cannot now locate. But we do know that he lived and ministered in the seventh century B.C. To understand his message, it helps to understand the political, military, and religious situation in that part of the world at that time.[2]

Text

The author sends a message, which is the text. In the case of biblical literature, the author is known only through the text. The intention of the author is hypothetically reconstructed through interaction with the text. Later we will see that this reconstructed author is the "implied" author. Interpretation thus calls for a close reading of the text. It calls for an acquaintance with the conventions and strategies of communication that guided the composition of the text.

I have noted Alter's comment that each culture or time period has its own conventions of literary communication. The primary task of the reader/critic is to recover these conventions and to learn their intended effect on the reader. Since the Bible did not come to us with an explicit analysis of its literary forms, we are frequently left to infer those conventions from our interaction with the text and must use etic rather than emic

---

intention of a particular passage of Scripture. This position further manifests itself in Kaiser's unwillingness to read Old Testament texts in the light of further New Testament revelation. Kaiser infers (p. 111) that true revelation must involve a complete and full disclosure on the part of God. In the light of 1 Peter 1:10–12, however, it is clear that the prophets wrote better than they knew (contra Kaiser). Since the reality of the New Testament relates to the shadows of the Old Testament, at some stage of their reading of the Old Testament, Christians appropriately avail themselves of that clearer revelation.

[2]See my forthcoming commentary on Nahum, to be published by Baker as part of a new series concentrating on the Minor Prophets.

categories. Chapters 4 and 6 will discuss these conventions for prose and poetry respectively.

Reader

From the standpoint of the reader we recognize that our readings are partial and contextualized. Application is part of the exegetical task. It is unwise and indeed impossible for readers to divest themselves completely of personal interests and concerns while reading. Indeed the Scriptures encourage readers to come to the text with their wholehearted commitment and needs. E. D. Hirsch and W. Kaiser wish to separate textual meaning from application, or significance. Although such a view may be fine in theory, it is impossible to implement fully in reality.

It is appropriate to make some distinctions when referring to the reader of the text. One may speak of the original reader, the later reader, and the implied reader. Traditional interpretation has concentrated on the original audience. How was the Gospel of Mark received by its first readers? This type of question is important and helps us to understand the ancient conventions of writing and the original intention of the author. The later reader refers to the history of interpretation and contemporary interpretations. The implied reader is a New Critical category and distinguishes the actual original readers from the readers addressed in the text itself.[3] The Book of Nahum once again provides a good example. The original readers of Nahum's prophecy were the inhabitants of Judah who were living under the vassalage of Assyria. The later readers include all subsequent commentators, including ourselves. The implied readers, then, were the Assyrians (though it is extremely unlikely that any Assyrian actually read it). Nahum addresses his prophecy to them, using taunt and satire.

In conclusion, literature is an act of communication

---

[3]G. Prince, "Introduction to the Study of the Narratee," in *Reader-Response Criticism,* ed. J. P. Tompkins (Baltimore: Johns Hopkins University Press, 1980), pp. 6–25.

between author and reader through a text. These three aspects of literature are interlocking and may not be abstracted from one another. Proper interpretation does not neglect any of the three.

FUNCTIONS OF BIBLICAL LITERATURE

As discussed in chapter 2, literary critics of the Bible all too frequently reduce the meaning of the biblical text to an aesthetic meaning. Literature, they say, does not refer outside of itself to external reality. Other scholars restrict the meaning of the biblical texts to their historical references.

Such positions result from a misunderstanding of the functions of literature in general and biblical literature in particular. The Bible is multifunctional. When viewed as an act of verbal communication from a sender to a receiver, the message of the text may be described as having many different purposes. With M. Sternberg, we may say, "Like all social discourse, biblical narrative is oriented to an addressee and regulated by a purpose or a set of purposes involving the addressee"; and with R. Jakobson, "Language must be investigated in all the variety of its functions."[4] While not intending to be exhaustive, I discuss here six major functions of biblical literature: historical, theological, doxological, didactic, aesthetic, and entertainment. Although I have isolated these functions from one another for the purpose of analysis, in the text they are all intertwined. Also, it is important to remember that the Bible contains a variety of literary types that vary in terms of the dominance of one or more of these functions.

Historical

As argued above, the Bible intends to impart historical information to its readers, primarily concerning the acts of God

---

[4]M. Sternberg, *The Poetics of Biblical Narrative* (Bloomington: Indiana University Press, 1985), p. 1; R. Jakobson, "Metalanguage as a Linguistic Problem," in *The Framework of Language* (Michigan Studies in the Humanities 1; Ann Arbor: University of Michigan, Department of Slavic Languages and Literatures, 1980), p. 81.

for and among His people. What I am calling the historical function of biblical literature may roughly be equated with what Jakobson terms the referential function of language.[5] Though most scholars today would not agree, I believe that this purpose is dominant in most biblical literature. The other functions are subsidiary in that they depend on the historical function.

In his recent volume on the poetics of biblical narrative, Sternberg provides a stimulating discussion of the historical function of biblical literature. He rightly points out that, ultimately, "nothing on the surface . . . infallibly marks off the two genres [fiction and history]." Nonetheless, he persuasively concludes that "the narrative is historiographic, inevitably so considering its teleology and incredibly so considering its time and environment. Everything points in this direction."[6] Sternberg's point stands whether the history is true or not. Biblical narrative, for the most part, *intends* to impart historical information.

Theological

The second function is closely related to the first. The Bible is not historical in a positivist, neutral sense; rather, it has a message to convey. What I am here calling theological, Sternberg labels ideological and Jakobson refers to as the emotive or expressive function of language. Jakobson describes the emotive function of language as that which "aims a direct expression of the speaker's attitude toward what he is speaking about."[7] The biblical storyteller as well as the biblical poet attributes the great events that happen in Israel to God. It intends to interpret that history in the light of the reality of God and His interaction with the world.

Doxological

Closely related to the theological function is the doxological purpose of the biblical text, a function that we could describe

---

[5] Jakobson, "Metalanguage," p. 82.
[6] Sternberg, *The Poetics,* p. 30.
[7] Jakobson, "Metalanguage," p. 82.

as partly theological and partly didactic. In short, the biblical authors intend to offer praise to God and to encourage the community to praise Him in response to the historical and theological truths that the text presents. Often this call to praise is implicit; at other times it is explicit (e.g., Exod. 15; Judg. 5).

Didactic

Biblical stories are often structured in order to shape the reader's ethical behavior. Jakobson similarly speaks of the connative function of language, which has its "orientation toward the addressee" and "finds its purest grammatical expression in the vocative and imperative."[8] Genesis 39, the story of Joseph and Potiphar's wife, is an excellent illustration. In this chapter Joseph is a virtual embodiment of the many proverbs that explicitly teach that young men should resist the advances of the strange or adulterous woman. A proper response to the story of Genesis 39 includes a chaste character on the part of the reader.

Aesthetic

In this book I concentrate particularly on the aesthetic function, but it is only one of many. Jakobson refers to the poetic function of all verbal communication as that function that is "set toward the message."[9] In other words, it concerns verbal self-reference. The aesthetic nature of the biblical text is observed in its self-consciousness about structure and language—about how the message is conveyed. It is seen in the indirection of the message (above also called distanciation). As Ryken comments specifically on the Gospels, "Instances from the life of Jesus such as these suggest a literary [or aesthetic] approach to truth that frequently avoids direct propositional statement and embodies truth in distinctly literary forms."[10]

[8]Ibid., p. 83.
[9]Ibid., p. 84.
[10]L. Ryken, *How to Read the Bible as Literature* (Grand Rapids: Zondervan, 1984), p. 9.

Entertainment

Biblical texts are shaped in a compelling way. They are enjoyable to read. This function is best seen in connection with the aesthetic function of the text.

It is essential to keep in mind the multifaceted nature of biblical literature. The danger of reducing the Bible to one or two functions is that it radically distorts the message as it comes from the ultimate sender (God) to us as its present receivers. The thrust of this book, however, is on the aesthetic function. Overall, then, my presentation is a partial analysis that must be supplemented by other forms of study.

Part 2

APPLICATION

4

THE ANALYSIS OF
PROSE PASSAGES

In this chapter I examine the nature of Hebrew narrative. Earlier we observed that all literature is conventional and that conventions differ, depending on time period and place of origin. It is of interest, therefore, to ask what characterizes Hebrew narrative. The following is not an exhaustive description of Hebrew prose but a beginning one intended to stimulate thought about particular passages. Neither is the following intended to be a step-by-step approach to the analysis of a passage from an aesthetic perspective. The concepts discussed here would be abused if applied in a mechanical fashion to biblical texts. In chapter 5, I analyze two prose sections of the Bible, 1 Kings 22:1–38 and Acts 10:1–11:18.

The reader must remember that a literary analysis is a partial analysis. It is best taken as an aspect of the historical-grammatical approach to the text; indeed, as L. Ryken points out, it is a "logical extension" of it.[1] A literary analysis will both highlight aspects of the passage that were previously unnoticed and also throw new light on the text as it is viewed from this different perspective.

The analysis of prose narrative will be presented under three subheadings. They are genre, the dynamics of narrative,

---

[1]Ryken, *The Bible as Literature,* p. 12.

and style. However, first prose narrative itself needs definition. Prose is best defined in contrast with poetry. Indeed, prose is often defined as nonpoetry—that is, as all discourse that does not display the traits of poetry. Since poetry awaits description in chapter 6, I must delay any adequate definition of prose until that time. Prose, though, is closer to ordinary speech than poetry and is structured by paragraphs rather than by lines and stanzas.

The adjective *narrative* distinguishes the prose under discussion as a special kind. Narration "suggests a communication process in which the narrative as message is transmitted by addresser to addressee" and emphasizes that there is a "succession of events." I tend to use the term synonymously with *story* though I am aware that there are differences.[2]

GENRE

I begin with genre for three reasons. First. the concept of genre describes the text as a whole.[3] Second, genre is, at least in part, an extrinsic analysis in that generic identification necessarily appeals to other texts. Third, genre, while treated in this chapter that concentrates on prose, is equally important in interpreting poetic passages.

What I here label genre analysis bears a close resemblance to form criticism. The major difference is that form criticism is a diachronic analysis, whereas genre analysis is synchronic, concerned to identify the type of literature, not its prehistory.

What Is a Genre?

The simplest definition of *genre* in literature is "a group of texts that bear one or more traits in common with each other." In the act of reading, as we have seen, a transaction takes place between the author and the reader, a transaction that is a form

---

[2] S. Rimmon-Kenan, *Narrative Fiction* (London: Methuen, 1983), pp. 2, 15.

[3] I use *genre* in this book to refer to a work as a whole and *form* to refer to a unit within a whole text.

of communication.[4] An adage instructs us that "the individual is ineffable."[5] That is, something that is totally unprecedented is incommunicable. In literary terms, a text that bears no similarities of structure, content, or the like with anything previously written cannot be understood by a reader.

Readers approach a text with certain expectations that arise as soon as they begin reading it and that are grounded in their previous reading. When they start to read a text, they make a conscious or unconscious genre identification, which involves further expectations concerning what is to come. Texts may trigger generic expectations in different ways. We pick up *The Hobbit* by J. R. R. Tolkien and read:

> In a hole in the ground there lived a hobbit. Not a nasty, dirty, wet hole, filled with the ends of worms and an oozy smell, nor yet a dry, bare, sandy hole with nothing in it to sit down on or to eat: it was a hobbit-hole, and that means comfort.[6]

Already certain expectations are formed in our minds. Since there are no such creatures as hobbits in the real world, we know we are moving in the realm of fiction, even fantasy. Indeed the cover of the version I have before me describes *The Hobbit* as "the enchanting prelude to 'The Lord of the Rings.'" This description strengthens our generic suspicions. Furthermore, if we have read the libretto to Richard Wagner's *Ring Cycle* or another story that uses the ring-of-power motif, additional expectations will be evoked in our minds.

Not only is genre recognizable in the expectations of the reader, but it also directs authors as they compose the text. It shapes or coerces writers so that their compositions can be grasped and communicated to the reader.[7]

---

[4]For more background on this approach and others, see K. Hempfer, *Gattungstheorie* (Munich: W. Funk, 1973). For a more detailed exposition of genre, consult Longman, "Form Criticism."

[5]See Buss, "The Study of Forms," p. 32; and R. Pascal, *Design and Truth in Autobiography* (Cambridge: Harvard University Press, 1960), p. 2.

[6]J. R. R. Tolkien, *The Hobbit* (New York: Ballentine, 1966), p. 15.

[7]G. Dillon, *Constructing Texts: Elements of a Theory of Composition and Style* (Bloomington: Indiana University Press, 1981); Wellek and Warren, *Theory of*

Genre theorists have offered a number of metaphors or models to describe genre. Chief among these theorists, R. Wellek and A. Warren speak of genre as an institution, similar to the state, university, or church.[8] An individual joins an institution, follows its rules and regulations in the main, but may opt to fight for change in either a subtle or radical manner. Moreover, an author may choose to play with the usual elements of a genre simply for satiric or other effects. A second metaphor is the legal contract. An author sets up an agreement with the readers concerning how the text should be read. T. Todorov imagines genre to be a code with the author as the encoder and the reader as the decoder.[9] Another metaphor enters genre theory via philosophy, specifically language philosophy. E. D. Hirsch draws on L. Wittgenstein's analogy of the sentence as a game. Just as a sentence is a game, so too is genre. In games there are rules, which shape the play of the game. His game analogy is apt, since language (syntax, diction, etc.) and genre also have rules that govern their successful operation.[10] These metaphors illuminate genre in three ways: genre explains the possibility of communication in a literary transaction; genres rest upon expectations that arise in readers when they confront a text; and authors can be coerced in composition to conform to genre expectations.

Fluid Concept of Genre

In the nineteenth century, genre theorists believed that genres were rigid and pure. Literary texts, it was felt, could be pigeonholed into their respective generic categories, and the

---

Literature, p. 226; and D. Kambouchner, "The Theory of Accidents," *Glyph* 7 (1980): 149–75.

[8] Wellek and Warren, *Theory of Literature,* p. 226.

[9] T. Todorov, *The Fantastic: A Structural Approach to a Literary Genre,* trans. R. Howard, with introduction by R. Scholes (Ithaca: Cornell University Press, 1974); cf. J. Culler, *The Pursuit of Signs* (Ithaca: Cornell University Press, 1981), pp. 11–12, 37.

[10] Hirsch, *Validity in Interpretation,* pp. 68–71; M. E. Amsler, "Literary Theory and the Genres of Middle English Literature," *Genre* 13 (1980): 389–90.

genres themselves could be arranged into hierarchies. Gunkel imported this unfortunate understanding of genre into biblical studies, though such a neoclassical position was already obsolete in his own day.[11] According to Gunkel, a particular text had one genre with a corresponding setting in life. Furthermore, so-called mixed genres (*Mischgattungen*) were considered late and corrupt.

In fact, such a position can be neither theoretically nor practically justified. Genre exists at all levels of generality. Genre, as stated above, refers to a class of texts united by the sharing of similarities, and thus it involves a generalization or abstraction from particular texts. It is, therefore, possible to speak of a broad genre of many texts with few traits in common, or of a narrow genre of as few as two texts that are identical in many ways. With Todorov, we thus speak of genres on a scale that ranges from one, in that all literature constitutes a single genre, to the maximum, that is where each text constitutes its own genre.[12] Such a notion of genre suggests that genres are not rigid categories.[13]

The fluidity of genre designations can be demonstrated by considering Psalm 98, a poem that may be classified in a variety of different genres, depending on the level of abstraction from the text itself.[14] It may be classified very broadly as a poem and have a few general similarities with other texts that we call poetry. On the other extreme, Psalm 98 may be classified narrowly in a genre with only Psalm 96. Psalm 96 is virtually identical to Psalm 98, with the exception that the former includes a diatribe against idol worship. Between these two extremes are a variety of other potential classifications for Psalm 98. Moving from broad to narrow, Psalm 98 may be treated as

---

[11] See Tucker, *Form Criticism,* pp. 4–5; and Buss, "The Study of Forms," p. 50.

[12] Hempfer, *Gattungstheorie,* p. 137.

[13] The Wittgensteinian concepts of "blurred edges" or "fuzzy concepts" are appropriate to describe the overlapping that does occur between genres; see Amsler, "Literary Theory," p. 390.

[14] For a more complete treatment, see my "Psalm 98: A Divine Warrior Hymn," *JETS* 27 (1984): 267–74.

a poem, a cultic hymn, a hymn concerning God's kingship, a divine-warrior victory psalm, and finally as most closely related to Psalm 96. One of the benefits of such a fluid approach to genre is that it demands that the exegete attend as closely to the peculiarities of the texts as to its similarities.

How to Classify a Text

Difficulty arises because texts do not identify themselves. Indeed, genre identification is a good example of the emic/etic problem raised in chapter 2. We do not have many native, or emic genre labels, so we must create etic categories that, while admittedly not found in the ancient materials, describe what we have in the text.

The only way to identify the genre of a text properly is to read it in the context of other, particularly biblical, literature and to note similarities between texts. Genre classification is a form of the hermeneutical circle in that it involves constant interaction between the particular text and the generalizing genre. The individual text can be grasped only through a knowledge of the whole. In short, genres can be elucidated only from the texts themselves.

Part of the confusion surrounding the identification of texts that cohere into a genre originates in unclarity concerning the kind of similarities among texts that signal that they belong to the same genre. Gunkel felt that a text could be generically classified according to three criteria: the mood and thought(s) of the text, the linguistic forms (grammar and vocabulary), and the social setting.[15]

This list is too restrictive. The best approach is to accept similarities between texts on many levels as evidence of generic identity. These similarities can be divided into inner form and outer form.[16] The outer form of a text includes the structure of the text and the meter (or its lack) in the speech rhythm. The

---

[15] H. Gunkel, *The Psalms* (Philadelphia: Fortress, 1967); Buss, "The Study of Forms," p. 1.

[16] Wellek and Warren, *Theory of Literature*, pp. 231–34.

inner form refers to the nonformal aspects of the texts—the mood, setting, function, narrative voice, and content. We can classify Psalm 98, for example, with Psalms 18, 47, 68, 93, and 96 as a single genre on the basis of the following characteristics:

Outer Form	Inner Form
Poetic style (parallelism, imagery, etc.)	Kingship theme (content)
	Praise (mood)
	Divine-warrior hymn (function)

Why Consider Genre?

Consciously or unconsciously, genre identification triggers what I have earlier called expectations on the part of the reader. Indeed it triggers a whole reading strategy. Consider the second stanza of Psalm 1:

> Not so the wicked!
>> They are like chaff
>> that the wind blows away.
> Therefore the wicked will not stand in the judgment,
>> nor sinners in the assembly of the righteous.

For various reasons, our interpretive strategy takes these lines as poetry. We expect the use of images and so forth (see chapter 6).

In another passage we read, "In the twelfth year of Ahaz king of Judah, Hoshea son of Elah became king of Israel in Samaria, and he reigned nine years" (2 Kings 17:1). Our immediate reaction is that this sentence is historical narrative, and we recognize that the author intends to communicate historical or chronological information.

We might have the same initial reaction to the following words of Jesus: "Two men went up to the temple to pray, one a Pharisee and the other a tax collector" (Luke 18:10). These words however, are preceded by "Jesus told this parable." Here we have an explicit generic signal that triggers a reading strategy that is significantly different from the one we adopt for the 2 Kings 17 passage. Jesus' story is fictional. More specifically, it is didactic fiction—that is, it intends to impart a moral to the hearer or reader.

N. Frye discusses insightfully a second value of generic criticism:

> The purpose of criticism by genres is not so much to classify as to clarify . . . traditions and affinities, thereby bringing out a large number of literary relationships that would not be noticed as long as there were no context established for them.[17]

In other words, the very practice of examining a collection of generically related texts will result in the illumination of each individual text. This result is particularly true of individual texts that are themselves difficult to understand but that may be elucidated by comparing them with clearer examples in the same genre.

Since the psalms are a collection of individual and separate texts, they have no normal literary context. More benefit may be gained by studying a psalm in the context of its genres than by examining the immediately preceding and following psalms. It is more fruitful, for example, to study Psalm 30 in the context of other thanksgiving hymns rather than in comparison with Psalms 29 and 31. For most other texts, insight is gained by studying both the immediate literary context and its generic context. For instance, Nahum 3:1–3 must be studied in its literary context (as occurring between two metaphorical taunts, 2:11–13 and 3:4–6). As a second essential step in understanding Nahum 3:1–3, the exegete must also compare and contrast it with all other occurrences of *hôy* oracles in the prophets and the historical books.

One frequently observed problem of the study of genre is its generalizing tendency. It concentrates on what is general or similar between texts, rather than on the uniqueness of each one. This imbalance is not inherent in the method, and indeed a genre analysis may be used to highlight the particular aspects of a psalm, since they will stand out in the context of the similarities of the texts.

---

[17] N. Frye, *Anatomy of Criticism* (Princeton: Princeton University Press, 1957), pp. 247–48.

For different reasons, then, it is important to discover the genre(s) of a text. By prompting a reading strategy and ruling out false expectations and standards of judgment of a text, genre classification represents an entrée to the meaning of the text.

THE DYNAMICS OF NARRATIVE

Up to this point, I have described the act of literary communication as involving three parts: author, text, and reader. The picture becomes more complex as we examine the story closely. The author does not make his or her presence known explicitly, and the reader is not referred to in the text. Critics interested in the working of literary narrative have made some important and helpful distinctions. They describe the interaction between author and audience using six terms:

Author → Implied Author → Narrator → Narratee → Implied Reader → Reader

I discuss in this section these terms and others that are important for describing narrative.[18]

Author/Reader

These terms require little explanation, since they are the most familiar to us. The author is the man or woman who actually composes the text, and the readers are those who actually read it. Of the six parts of the act of literary communication, the author and the reader are the only ones outside of the narrative itself.

Problems confront the biblical scholar at this point, however. It is likely that sources were used in the composition of certain biblical books, and it is possible that other books underwent some sort of editorial revision. Should we speak of one author, many authors, or even many editors?

For the purposes of literary analysis, this question is relatively unimportant. I do not deny that diachronic analysis

---

[18] For a discussion and further bibliography, consult Culpepper, *Anatomy*, pp. 6ff.

may have its place, but for the purposes of a literary analysis, the question is at least momentarily set aside.

The question of the reader is also complicated, particularly in the study of an ancient text. Readers of biblical texts span centuries. One of the goals of traditional historical-grammatical exegesis is to answer the question, how did the *original* readers understand the passage? This question is valid and must be answered. Twentieth-century men and women, however, are readers too. We are distanced from the text in a way that the original readers were not. That is, we come with different questions and also have lost touch with some of the conventions of biblical literature. I therefore propose separating *reader* into original reader and contemporary reader. The goal of the contemporary reader is to understand the text by means of its ancient conventions, but such a reader approaches the text through a new grid of questions that are evoked by the situation of modern society and culture (see chapter 3).

Implied Author/Implied Reader

The distinction between, on the one hand, the implied author and implied reader and, on the other hand, the actual author and actual reader is a difficult one to express. Sometimes, it must be admitted, it is of little practical import to the analysis of a biblical text. The distinction is a real one, though. The implied author is the textual manifestation of the real author. Rimmon-Kenan states the matter very clearly: "The implied author is the governing consciousness of the work as a whole, the source of the norms embodied in the work."[19] *The implied author is the author as he or she would be constructed, based on inference from the text.* The work may contain and advocate beliefs and opinions that the real author does not actually hold. Although the distinction is theoretically valid, it becomes academic in many or most biblical books because our sole

---

[19]Rimmon-Kenan, *Narrative Fiction,* p. 86. The concept of implied author was to my knowledge first developed by W. Booth, *The Rhetoric of Fiction* (Chicago: University of Chicago Press, 1961), pp. 71–76, 211–21.

knowledge of the author is reconstructed from the text. In cases in which the narrator provides the structure to the whole and carries the author's viewpoint, the implied author is related to the narrator.

As one might expect, the implied reader, on analogy with the implied author, is not a real but an imaginary figure. S. Chatman provides a helpful description of the implied reader: "The *implied reader*—not the flesh-and-bones you or I sitting in our living rooms reading the book, but the audience presupposed by the narrative itself."[20]

Narrator/Narratee

Perhaps the most fruitful of the above three pairs for narrative analysis is the narrator/narratee. Both narrator and narratee are rhetorical devices and are often explicit in the text, though they both may take different forms from text to text. In general, the narrator is the one who tells the story and the narratee is the one who hears it. The narrator is most obviously seen when he or she is a character (for instance, Serenus Zeitblom in *Doctor Faustus,* by Thomas Mann) but is no less true when the narrator is not a character and is unnamed (the narrator of *Jude the Obscure,* by Thomas Hardy).

A description of the role of the narrator in a story is closely related to the issue of point of view, a topic I discuss in the next section. The narrator plays a pivotal role in shaping the reaction of the reader to the passage he or she is reading. The narrator achieves this response in a variety of ways, from presenting and withholding information from the reader to explicit commentary.

Narratives may be divided into first- and third-person narratives. In the former, the narrator is usually a character in the story and, as a result, presents a limited point of view. Third-person narrative refers to all the characters impersonally, and in this mode the narrator may display omniscience and

---

[20] S. Chatman, *Story and Discourse* (Ithaca: Cornell University Press, 1978), pp. 149–50.

omnipresence. Note that most narrative in the Bible is third-person omniscient narrative (the exceptions include part of Nehemiah, Qohelet's "autobiography" in Ecclesiastes, and the "we" passages in Acts.) Rhoads and Michie, for example, describe such a narrator and point of view in the Gospel of Mark:

> The narrator does not figure in the events of the story; speaks in the third person; is not bound by time or space in the telling of the story; is an implied invisible presence in every scene, capable of being anywhere to "recount" the action; displays full omniscience by narrating the thoughts, feelings, or sensory experiences of many characters; often turns from the story to give direct "asides" to the reader, explaining a custom or translating a word or commenting on the story; and narrates the story from one overarching ideological point of view.[21]

This summary describes the bulk of biblical narrative. The voice of the narrator is often the authoritative guide in the story, directing the reader in his or her analysis and response to the events and characters of the story.

It has been pointed out that readers react to a third-person omniscient narrator with an unconscious submissiveness. Rhoads and Michie note, "When the narrator is omniscient and invisible, readers tend to be unaware of the narrator's biases, values, and conceptual view of the world."[22] The choice of such a powerfully persuasive literary device fits in with the Bible's concern to proclaim an authoritative message.

The narratee, simply, is the person or group addressed by the narrator.[23] The narratee may or may not be a character in the text. In the Gospel of Luke, for instance, the narratee is Theophilus. An interesting book to which to apply the concept of the narratee is Nahum. The original readers were no doubt Judeans. The implied readers were faithful Judeans who desired the destruction of Nineveh. The narratee, however, is the Ninevites. It is doubtful whether the Ninevites ever read the

---

[21] Rhoads and Michie, *Mark as Story,* p. 36.
[22] Ibid., p. 39.
[23] Prince, "Introduction," pp. 7–25.

book, but the narrator (and here narrator, implied author, and real author are impossible to distinguish) addresses the book to the Ninevites.

Point of View

The analogy with film is helpful toward understanding point of view in literature. In a film, the eye of the camera grants perspective as it moves from place to place, coming in for a close-up here and then panning to another shot. The camera guides and limits the audience's insight.

As mentioned, point of view in literature is closely bound with the narrator. He is the one who mediates perspective on the characters and the events of the story. He guides readers in their interpretation of those characters and events and, through his manipulation of the point of view, draws readers into the story. Literary scholars have proposed different approaches to the description and categorization of point of view in narrative. The most fruitful is that of Boris Uspensky, who distinguishes five different "planes" of point of view: spatial, temporal, phraseological, psychological, and ideological.[24] Four of these planes are clearly important for the literary analysis of biblical texts.

Spatial. If the narrator is identified with a particular character, then quite often the narrator is localized. Otherwise, the narrator may be omnipresent, jumping from scene to scene, present where a character could not be. The latter is found far more frequently in biblical literature. In Joshua 5:13–15, the narrator is present with Joshua as he confronts the commander of the army of the Lord. In 2 Samuel 11, the narrator is with David as he is walking alone on his roof and notices Bathsheba.

Temporal. This term refers to the temporal limitation (or lack of it) imposed on the narrator. Is the narrator confined to telling the story as it unfolds—that is, as he witnesses it? Or

---

[24]B. Uspensky, *A Poetics of Composition* (Berkeley: University of California Press, 1973). Note the stimulating application of Uspensky's work to biblical literature in Berlin, *Poetics and Interpretation,* pp. 55–56.

possibly is the narrator telling the story at a later period of time and thus has information concerning the conclusion of a chain of events? Or is the narrator able to transcend time? In the Book of Esther, the narrator is third person and is omnipresent and omniscient, but temporally he does not anticipate the future, following the events as they unfold. This feature certainly enhances the suspense of the story.

Psychological. Does the narrator report the thoughts and emotions of the characters? Can he penetrate their inner life? If so, then the narrator is omniscient, providing information to which no character has access.

Ideological. The final category is the most interesting. Ideological point of view concerns evaluation by the narrator. In this plane the narrator guides the readers' interpretation of events.

The message of a prose narrative in Scripture may be better understood by closely questioning the text concerning the narrator and his point of view. The four aspects considered in this section provide a useful categorization of point of view.

Character

Some readers may hesitate at this point. Should we treat David, Solomon, Ezra, Esther, Jonah—even Jesus—as characters? Such a move appears to equate biblical personages with King Arthur, Billy Budd, Felix Holt, or Captain Ahab and thus to reduce them to fictional beings.

Indeed some advocates of the literary approach do so and rejoice that they have skirted the historical issue. In my view, however, to analyze David as a literary character in a text is not to deny that he was a historical king or that the events reported in the books of Samuel and Kings are accurate. We must admit, however, that we have a selective account of the life of David and can agree that there is value in taking a close look at how the text portrays David and others. In other words, we must recognize that our accounts are shaped—that is, we have in the Bible selective, emphasized, and interpreted accounts of historical events.

We do not get a full report of the events of the life of Jesus, as John explicitly admits for his gospel: "Jesus did many other things as well. If every one of them were written down, I suppose that even the whole world would not have room for the books that would be written" (21:25). The immediately preceding verse indicates that the selective nature of his account did not impinge on its truthfulness: "This is the disciple who testifies to these things and who wrote them down. We know that his testimony is true" (v. 24).

The essential point is that a literary, in this case a characterological, analysis is partial. Although the focus of such research is not on the historical dimension of the text, still this dimension must in no way be ignored or rejected. Otherwise we would be trifling with the text and not taking seriously its original purpose.

The modern interpreter must understand the conventional means of characterization in Hebrew narrative. In the first place, the Bible rarely describes its characters.[25] We do not have any extensive physical or psychological descriptions of biblical characters. If such a detail is given, it is usually of great importance in the story. We are told at an appropriate place that Saul was "a head taller than any of the others" (1 Sam. 9:2), that Bathsheba was "very beautiful" (2 Sam. 11:2), that Ehud was left-handed (Judg. 3:15), and that Samson was strong and had long hair (Judg. 13–16). But such comments are isolated, of significance to the rest of the story.

This feature is strikingly different from nineteenth-century English authors, who describe their characters explicitly and with painstaking detail. Note the description of Denner, a rather minor character, in the opening of George Eliot's *Felix Holt:*

---

[25] This fact has been noticed in modern times at least since E. Auerbach's well-known judgment that biblical stories are "fraught with background" (*Mimesis* [Princeton: Princeton University Press, 1953], p. 12). R. Alter, A. Berlin, and M. Sternberg are among the most notable commentators on this phenomenon of biblical style.

> Denner had still strong eyes of that shortsighted kind which see through the narrowest chink between the eyelashes. The physical contrast between the tall, eagle-faced, dark-eyed lady, and the little peering waiting-woman, who had been round-featured and of pale mealy complexion from her youth up, had doubtless had a strong influence in determining Denner's feeling towards her mistress.[26]

Furthermore, we are rarely given motives for the behavior of biblical characters. In Genesis 22 we are not told what Abraham is feeling or how he rationalized God's command to sacrifice Isaac. What was going through Gideon's mind when he made the golden ephod (Judg. 8:25–27)? The narrator's judgment is not totally lacking in biblical stories, but it is rare.

Alter's careful study of biblical characterization deserves lengthy quotation:

> Now, in reliable third-person narrations, such as in the Bible, there is a scale of means, in ascending order of explicitness and certainty, for conveying information about the motives, the attitudes, the moral nature of characters. Character can be revealed through the report of actions; through appearance, gestures, posture, costume; through one character's comments on another; through direct speech by the character; through inward speech, either summarized or quoted as interior monologue; or through statements by the narrator about the attitudes and intentions of the personages, which may come either as flat assertions or motivated explanations.[27]

Such characterization has significant consequences for interpretation. It means that we generally have only indirect description of characters and motivations for their actions. The interpreter must sometimes read between the lines to round out the picture (see below on gapping). Without indulging in wholesale speculation and eisegesis, the reader must make inferences from the text about characters and in fact is encouraged to do so by the text.

---

[26] G. Eliot, *Felix Holt* (New York: Penguin, 1972), p. 102.
[27] Alter, *The Art of Biblical Narrative*, pp. 116–17.

In Bruce Waltke's illuminating study of the Cain and Abel story (Gen. 4), he applies some of Alter's insights into the nature of biblical characterization.[28] The question over the rejection of Cain's sacrifice has plagued readers of the Bible for centuries. Was Cain's sacrifice unacceptable because it was not a bloody sacrifice? Or was it rejected because it was not offered in faith? The enigma of Cain's sacrifice has arisen because of the silence of the Old Testament text concerning Cain's motives for bringing his sacrifice and God's motives for rejecting it. The text introduces Cain and Abel very abruptly and tells only briefly the story leading up to Abel's murder.

Waltke points to indirect indications within the text that help solve the problem. Generally speaking, the passage becomes clearer once it is realized that the text contrasts Cain and Abel's actions. Alter highlights character contrast as a favorite device of Hebrew narrative. Waltke notices two important differences in terms of the sacrifice that each brother brought. The narrator mentions that Abel brought the "firstborn" of the flock, whereas Cain's sacrifice from the "fruits of the soil" is not specified as the equivalent of "firstfruits." Abel offered the "fat," which is the best part of the animal, whereas Cain's sacrifice is not qualified in any equivalent way. Waltke's conclusion seems warranted: "Abel's sacrifice is characterized as the best of its class and . . . Cain's is not. The point seems to be that Abel's sacrifice represents heartfelt worship; Cain's represents unacceptable tokenism."[29]

Biblical literary critics find it useful to make distinctions between round and flat characters and what have been called agents. Berlin defines this threefold categorization and provides examples, particularly from the David narrative.[30] A round (or full-fledged) character has many traits. A round character appears complex, less predictable, and therefore more real. A flat character has only one trait and seems one-dimensional. An agent, finally, has no personality to speak of and simply moves

---

[28] B. Waltke, "Was Cain's Offering Rejected by God Because It Was Not a Blood Sacrifice?" *WTJ* 48 (1986): 363–72.

[29] Ibid., p. 369.

[30] Berlin, *Poetics and Interpretation*, pp. 23–33.

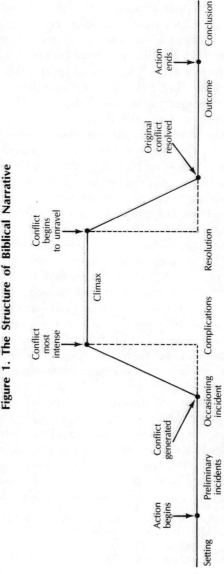

Figure 1. The Structure of Biblical Narrative

the story along. Examples of these three character types will be given in the next chapter.

Plot

Plot and character are closely related and may be separated only for purposes of analysis. Henry James related the two elements by asking, "What is character but the determination of incident? What is incident but the illustration of character?"[31] The debates over whether plot or character is prior seem ill-founded, since they are interdependent and equally important.

Descriptions of the dynamics of plot differ in detail between literary critics. The first and simplest is Aristotle's; he describes a plot as having a beginning, middle, and end.[32] P. Brooks defines plot in the following helpful way: "Plot is the principle of interconnectedness and intention which we cannot do without in moving through the discrete elements—incidents, episodes, actions—of a narrative."[33]

Poythress provides a more sophisticated analysis of narrative, which may be represented graphically as in figure 1.[34] The analyses of the next chapter will apply this model of plot description to particular passages.

As a general rule, plot is thrust forward by conflict. The conflict generates interest in its resolution. The beginning of a story, with its introduction of conflict, thus pushes us through the middle toward the end, when conflict is resolved.[35]

One other helpful distinction in the analysis of a story's plot is that between *fabula* and *sjužet*. "*Fabula* is defined as the

[31] Quoted in Chatman, *Story and Discourse*, pp. 112–13.

[32] K. A. Telford, *Aristotle's Poetics: Translation and Analysis* (South Bend, Ind.: Gateway Editions, 1961), p. 15.

[33] P. Brooks, *Reading for the Plot: Design and Intention in Narrative* (New York: Vintage Books, 1984), p. 5.

[34] I am indebted to L. Newell for bringing this model to my attention. The model itself is the work of V. Poythress, based on the work of J. Beekman, "The Semantic Structure of Written Communication" (Dallas: Summer Institute of Linguistics, unpublished paper).

[35] For a more sophisticated statement of this view of plot, see Brooks's discussion of "narrative desire" (*Reading for the Plot*, pp. 37–61).

order of events referred to by the narrative, whereas *sjužet* is the order of events presented in the narrative discourse."[36] This distinction provides a tool for the analysis of dischronologized narrative in the Bible.

Setting

Setting is also related to plot and character. The characters live and act, with the setting providing the background. The setting provides the physical location of the action, sometimes adds atmosphere, and at other times supports the message of the passage.

The settings of literary texts are sometimes real places, sometimes imaginary, sometimes a mixture. *Typee,* by Herman Melville, is set on a South Seas island; *The Hobbit* in the fictitious Middle Earth. Boccaccio's *Decameron* is a complex of numerous short stories, set in many different locales, but the frame of the story is set in Florence, Italy, in A.D. 1349. The setting of *The Decameron* contributes to the atmosphere of the story, since that place at that time was subject to the ravages of a horrible plague.

Setting is an important aspect of the biblical story. Again, to focus on setting is not to denigrate the historical basis of the story. A clear example of the importance of setting in the interpretation of the biblical text is the Sermon on the Mount. An interesting point here is the variation in setting between the accounts in Matthew and in Luke. In Luke the sermon is delivered on a level place (Luke 6:17); in Matthew Jesus is on a mountainside (Matt. 5:1). Harmonization is possible between the two accounts, but the question must be asked, Why does Matthew choose to report the sermon as taking place on a mountain? The answer comes as we recognize that Matthew repeatedly draws analogies between the life of Jesus and the Exodus, wilderness wanderings, and conquest of the Old Testament. In Matthew's account, after Jesus returns from forty days in the wilderness, he ascends the mountain where he talks

---

[36] Ibid., p. 12.

about the law of God. Who can miss it? Jesus' preaching on the law on the mount is related to Moses' receiving the law on Mount Sinai.

STYLE

The third major subdivision of our analysis of prose narrative is style. We could examine style from a variety of levels. For instance, each individual writer has his or her own particular way of writing. In this chapter, however, we are concerned with a miscellany of items that characterize biblical style as a whole. Once again, the purpose is not to be exhaustive, but suggestive.

Many definitions of style have been proposed, but that of Leech and Short is clear and helpful, though couched in terms of individual style: "Every writer necessarily makes choices of expression, and it is in these choices, in his 'way of putting things,' that style resides. . . . Every analysis of style . . . is an attempt to find the artistic principles underlying a writer's choice of language."[37]

Repetition

Repetition is particularly noticeable in Old Testament narrative. Repetition in poetry has long been observed and categorized (see chapter 6). Prose too is repetitive. The scholarly reaction to repetition in prose, however, has usually been to defend source analysis. According to traditional biblical criticism, literary redundancy, either exact or more frequently partial, arises as the result of the merging of separate documents with one another. Advocates of a literary approach, on the other hand, are open to explaining repetition as a feature of Hebrew narrative style. Instead of weeding out redundancies, scholars thus pay close attention to the way in which repetitions function in the text.

---

[37] G. N. Leech and M. H. Short, *Style in Fiction* (London: Longman, 1981), pp. 19, 74.

Alter provides a kind of typology of repetitions in the Hebrew Bible.[38] He identified five types of repetitions: *Leitwort,* motif, theme, sequence of actions, and type-scene. Leitwort and type-scene are two types of repetition that are characteristic of the Bible and deserve special comment here.

Leitwort: In certain texts a particular word or words have prominence by virtue of frequent and strategic use. For instance, in 2 Samuel 7, which describes the establishment of a covenant between David and the Lord, the word *house* (*bayit*) takes on special significance. David wished to build a house (temple) for the Lord, especially since he has just built a house (palace) for himself. God does not permit David to do so; however, God will build a house (dynasty) for David. Identifying such words helps the exegete discover the structure and emphasis in a passage of Scripture.

Type-scene: Alter develops this term to describe texts that are similar in content and structure, or "an episode occurring at a portentous moment in the career of the hero which is composed of a fixed sequence of motifs."[39] J. G. Williams has studied the type-scene of barren women who give birth to boys who become biblical heroes.[40]

There is a growing tendency in biblical scholarship to accept repetitions in biblical narrative as part of the text and not to excise them as indications of conflated texts. Indeed a close reading of passages to detect variation between doublets brings additional insight to the understanding of a passage. Particular sensitivity should be directed toward the minute variations that occur between generally repetitious lines.

Omission

Another stylistic characteristic of biblical texts, almost the opposite of repetition, is omission. The study of omission has received concentrated attention in recent secondary literature on

---

[38] Alter, *The Art of Biblical Narrative,* pp. 95–113.

[39] Ibid., p. 96.

[40] J. G. Williams, "The Beautiful and the Barren: Conventions in Biblical Type-Scenes," *JSOT* 17 (1980): 107–19.

prose narrative and has also been labeled "gapping" or "narrative reticence." Much of Meir Sternberg's work accentuates the major importance of gapping in Hebrew storytelling. He speaks of a "system of gaps" that constitutes a literary (biblical) work.[41]

Quite simply, a gap is an unstated piece of information that is essential to the understanding of a story, for instance, an unstated motive (see above under "Character"). Why did Uriah not sleep with his wife when he was called home from the front lines by David? Did he suspect David's plan, or was he observing certain holy-war provisions that included not sleeping with a woman before a battle? Uriah himself states the latter, but is he telling David his true motive? Motives are not the only omissions in the stories of the Bible. We are also left wondering about causes, purposes, and so forth. On many occasions we would be happier if the biblical narrator would have been explicit in terms of moral evaluation of some actions and characters.

The phenomenon of gaps in the biblical story is an important one for readers to recognize, although some scholars have overemphasized it. We observed above how a scholar such as the deconstructionist Miscall can exploit gaps to introduce a fundamental and unresolvable "undecidability" to texts. While we must reckon with intentional ambiguity, a close reading of the text will allow the reader to close the gap correctly.

The phenomenon of gapping may be explained partly as a function of the necessary selectivity of the story. Since some of the omissions are seemingly crucial toward the proper understanding of a text, gapping plays other roles. Sternberg has correctly identified a second major function in that gaps involve the reader by raising "narrative interest: curiosity, suspense, surprise."[42]

Irony

Irony, like metaphor (see chapter 6), is a focus of recent discussion in literary criticism. Both irony and metaphor are

---

[41] Sternberg, *The Poetics,* p. 186.

[42] Ibid., p. 259.

figures of speech in that they "cannot be understood without rejecting what they seem to say."[43] Also, many exaggerated claims have been made about both of these figures, including the premises that all good literature is ironic or metaphorical. Since irony is frequently encountered in literature, including biblical literature, sensitive readers of the Scriptures must be able to recognize and interpret it.

The most lucid and helpful discussion of irony to be found today is that of Wayne Booth, upon whose work I am primarily dependent. Booth makes an important distinction between stable irony and unstable irony, of which only the former appears in the Bible. Booth describes stable irony as sharing four characteristics. First, it is *intended* by the author. The ironic author asserts "something in order to have it rejected as false."[44] Of course, this view involves a hypothesis about an unstated intention of the author, but Booth points out that stable ironies are almost always easily recognized as such. Then stable irony is *covert*. The implied author and narrator are silent about the ironic nature of a statement or passage. Ironies are "intended to be reconstructed with meanings different from those on the surface."[45] Third, biblical ironies are *stable* in that there is a limit to how deeply they displace the surface meaning of the text. Finally, such ironies are limited in terms of scope, treating only a certain part of the text as ironic. In Booth's terms they are *local,* or *finite*.

Following his definition of stable irony, Booth neatly describes how the sensitive reader reacts as he or she encounters an ironic statement or passage. He summarizes "Four Steps of Reconstruction." The first step involves the necessary rejection of the surface, or plain, meaning of a text, which might arise because of a direct signal from the author, a patently false position being proclaimed as truth, "conflicts of fact within the work," or some other signal. All of these devices may be

---

[43] W. Booth, *The Rhetoric of Irony* (Chicago: University of Chicago Press, 1974), p. 1.

[44] D. C. Muecke, *Irony and the Ironic* (Critical Idiom 13; London: Methuen, 1970), p. 56.

[45] Booth, *The Rhetoric of Irony,* p. 6.

summed up as the belief that "if the author did not intend irony, it would be odd, or outlandish, or inept, or stupid of him to do things in this way."[46] Then, after rejecting the literal meaning of a passage, the possibility that the author was careless must be taken into account. This attitude involves, third, a hypothesis concerning the author's "knowledge or belief." Finally, a new meaning is chosen.

Irony has long been recognized as a literary device in the Bible. Indeed one of the first monographs written from a distinctively literary perspective was the book *Irony in the Old Testament*.[47] Recent work has concentrated on the fourth Gospel, with many beneficial results.[48] Irony is a particularly effective device to demolish self-satisfied and proud positions and peoples by exposing their blindness. The smug Pharisees and religious leaders of Israel are shown to be oblivious to the obvious by the use of irony throughout the gospel. The most striking and significant irony is their execution of Jesus with the intention of ridding the world of His influence. His death brought the church to life; indeed through death, life triumphs.

Dialogue

The last element of biblical style to be discussed here is the role of dialogue in biblical storytelling. Dialogue plays a major part in the narrative of the Bible, and the recent secondary literature includes some helpful descriptions of it. The work of Alter and Berlin is particularly insightful; much that follows is dependent on them.[49]

In reading stories in the Bible, one quickly recognizes the high proportion of dialogue to narrative. In 1 Samuel 20, for instance, dialogue between David and Jonathan begins and ends

[46]Ibid., pp. 61, 52–53.

[47]E. M. Good, *Irony in the Old Testament* (Sheffield: Almond, 1981; orig. Philadelphia: Westminster, 1965).

[48]Culpepper, *Anatomy*, pp. 165–80; see also P. Duke, *Irony in the Fourth Gospel* (Atlanta: John Knox, 1985).

[49]Alter, *The Art of Biblical Narrative*, pp. 63–87; Berlin, *Poetics and Interpretation*, pp. 64–72.

the chapter, while a dialogue between Jonathan and Saul is found in the center. The narrative in this chapter functions to change the setting (e.g., vv. 24–25) or to provide "a bridge between much larger units of direct speech."[50]

In this brief section, only a few general characteristics of the conventions governing the presentation and function of dialogue may be given. Illustrations will come in the next chapter. As Alter has emphasized, dialogue almost invariably occurs between two characters, rarely three or more. One or both of the characters may be a group speaking as one person or actually speaking through a spokesman (1 Kings 12). The two characters engaged in dialogue are often contrasted with one another. Their styles of speech differ and serve to characterize a biblical personality. In his analysis of Genesis 25, Alter contrasts "Esau's inarticulate outbursts over against Jacob's calculated legalisms."[51] In general, the frequent use of dialogue in biblical narrative effects a strong measure of realism and vividness. With Berlin, it is possible to say, "Direct speech . . . is the most dramatic way of conveying the characters' internal psychological and ideological points of view."[52]

---

[50] Alter, *The Art of Biblical Narrative*, p. 65.

[51] Ibid., p. 72.

[52] Berlin, *Poetics and Interpretation*, p. 64.

5

EXAMPLES OF
PROSE ANALYSIS

Having examined in general how to approach a prose
narrative in the Bible, we now apply our study to two particular
narratives. I consider here the account of King Ahab's demise
and the record of the Gentiles' entrance into the early church.[1]

1 KINGS 22:1–38: GOD ENDS AHAB'S REIGN

I have chosen this particular story partly because literary
theorists are naturally attracted to passages from Genesis and
Samuel and have produced far fewer studies that are based on
texts found in Kings or Chronicles. More positively, the story
of Micaiah and Ahab is a stirring and self-contained plot. Of
course, it is part of the larger Ahab narrative, which means that,
by the time we come to 1 Kings 22, Ahab is a prominent
figure. Another advantage of taking one of our examples from
the Book of Kings is that we can compare it with the parallel
story in the Book of Chronicles (2 Chron. 18). As we do so,
we will see how close certain aspects of aesthetic criticism are to

---

[1] A previous literary analysis of 1 Kings 22 is by D. Robertson, "Micaiah ben
Imlah: A Literary View," in *The Biblical Mosaic: Changing Perspectives,* ed. R. M
Polzin and E. Rothman (Philadelphia: Fortress, 1982), pp. 139–46. I found
Robertson's work very unhelpful.

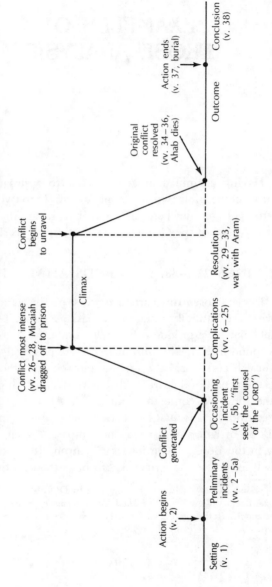

Figure 2. The Structure of Biblical Narrative: 1 Kings 22:1-38

redaction criticism, particularly while identifying the point of view of the narrator in each version.

As mentioned before, all of the separate elements that we identified in the dynamics of prose narrative are actually interrelated. The descriptions of narrator, point of view, and the other dynamics of story are separated only for pedagogical reasons. Indeed the overlap between the various elements will be apparent from the start.

Plot

Rather than giving a traditional plot summary that would simply paraphrase the sequence of events as they appear in the story, I use the plot line as presented above. (See fig. 2.) The account in Chronicles differs at the beginning and the end; the middle remains essentially the same. Nonetheless, the variation has important implications for the interpretation of the story. Chronicles focuses on Jehoshaphat rather than Ahab. Moreover, the Judean king's culpability is greatly heightened in Chronicles.

The plot may be traced by means of the conflict between characters in the story. This function of plot is not unusual. As Ryken aptly points out, "The essence of plot is a central conflict or set of conflicts moving toward a resolution."[2] At least three clashes occur in 1 Kings 22. The first is the war between Israel and Aram, the conflict that provides the setting for the other two and for all the action that takes place. The second conflict is between Micaiah and Zedekiah, the latter representing all of the false prophets and the former representing Yahweh's chosen messenger. The third and most important conflict is between Ahab and Micaiah. Ahab, as in the earlier narratives concerning his reign, represents the apostate people of God. Micaiah represents Yahweh. Indeed the conflict between Ahab and Micaiah is ultimately a conflict between the king of Israel and God Himself.

The narrative tension increases once Jehoshaphat requests

---

[2] Ryken, *The Bible as Literature,* p. 40.

that Ahab obtain a holy-war oracle. The Judean king persists until they hear an authentic word of the Lord from Micaiah. The tension escalates dramatically as the kings ignore the oracle and prepare for war. Ahab fights the oracle to the utmost by entering the battle in disguise and without his royal regalia and by inducing Jehoshaphat, who is likely a lesser treaty partner, to attract the attention of the enemy.

The plot finds its resolution as the arrow finds its target in the gaps of Ahab's armor and he eventually dies. The conflict between Ahab and God is thus the only one that finds explicit resolution in the story. The narrator is not concerned to inform us about the outcome of the struggle with Aram. Furthermore, we infer from events that Micaiah won the conflict with Zedekiah, though we hear nothing from the true prophet after he is dragged off to prison.

Genre

Genre, as argued above, is a fluid concept. First Kings 22 could thus be classified as a number of different genres from narrow to broad. Briefly, the narrative that focuses on Ahab and Micaiah may broadly be called *didactic history*. As a matter of fact, most of Kings and most, if not all, of the historical books in the Old Testament may be so labeled. First Kings 22 is didactic in two ways. First, it fits into the overall purpose of the Deuteronomic History to explain why Israel is now in exile. Second, it teaches the reader to avoid evil behavior (defined here as fleeing from Yahweh's law and will) as it is embodied in Ahab.

More specifically, however, 1 Kings 22 is a *prophetic story* or *prophetic history*. In other words, it is one of many episodes that center on the ministry of a prophet. In this case, the plot revolves around conflicting prophetic words and may be called a *prophetic contest story,* bearing a relationship to other texts in which prophets present conflicting oracles or represent different deities (chaps. 13, 18, etc.).[3]

---

[3]For other views on the genre of this story, see S. J. DeVries, *Prophet Against Prophet: The Role of the Micaiah Narrative (I Kings 22) in the Development of Early*

Narrator

We come to know the narrator in 1 Kings 22 not only from his intrusive comments but also from his management of the dialogue. Nevertheless, he guides our attitudes toward the events and the characters of the story primarily through his explicit comments. The narrator is unnamed and not a character. He speaks of all the characters in the third person. His intrusive comments come at the beginning and end of scenes. Otherwise he permits the characters to speak for themselves. The narrator is omnipresent. He is a presence hovering in the king's council chambers (1 Kings 22:3), in the gate in Samaria (vv. 10–12), and in the Aramean camp (vv. 31–33). He is also with the messenger who summons Micaiah (v. 13).

The narrator is omniscient. However, during the first part and middle part of the plot, the narrator does not demonstrate his omniscience. He functions more like a tape recorder present on the scene in order to pick up conversations. There is even a minimum of interpretive comments in this center part of the story. Indeed evidence that exposes the omniscience of the narrator in this story is slight. But it surfaces at a crucial spot in the narrative. From some English translations of verse 32, it might be inferred that the narrator is reading the minds of the chariot commanders. For instance, the NIV translates the main verb of the verse "they thought." The verb (from ' $\bar{a}mar$), however, is better translated "they said" and therefore does not presuppose omniscience on the part of the narrator. The narrator's omniscience, though restrained, becomes manifest only in verse 34 in the comment that the arrow that killed Ahab was drawn at random. This comment assumes knowledge on the part of the narrator of the thought processes of the archer.

Ideological viewpoint provides an intersection between literary criticism and redaction criticism. Since the narrator is the literary device by which readers are guided in their interpretation of the events of the story, the analysis of the

Prophetic Tradition (Grand Rapids: Eerdmans, 1978); idem, *I Kings* (Word 12; Waco, Tex.: Word, 1985), pp. 265–72; B. O. Long, *I Kings, with an Introduction to Historical Literature* (FOTL 9; Grand Rapids; Eerdmans, 1984), pp. 230–40.

ideology of the narrator leads to a determination of the theological *Tendenz* of the passage, one of the goals of redaction criticism.

In the Kings version of the story, we find explicit ideological commentary by the narrator in verses 37–38. These two verses highlight the moral of the story that the prophetic word of judgment against Ahab has been fulfilled. In Chronicles Ahab is really a minor character (see below). The narrator is not concerned about the king of Israel; rather, he concentrates on Jehoshaphat. The narrator thus omits the explicit commentary on Ahab at the end of the story and substitutes a speech by Jehu, a prophet, which draws the moral. In brief, the moral is that Jehoshaphat has sinned because he was drawn into evil through a treaty alliance with the northern kingdom. Nonetheless, Jehoshaphat also receives qualified praise for his interest in cultic purity.

Characterization

In this Ahab story, perhaps surprisingly, no character is presented as a psychologically complex person. They all appear as single- or double-trait characters or as agents who have no traits but simply carry the plot along.

Ahab. The obvious possible exception to this generalization about characterization is Ahab. He is introduced as a character as early as 1 Kings 16:28. There is more textual material on him than any other king except David and Solomon. As the reader proceeds, however, he or she may be surprised at how little the narrator reveals about Ahab or his motivations, beyond the fact that he is evil. Of course, the demonstration of his evil nature is most important for the moral of the story.

The one minor exception to this description of Ahab's characterization comes in the story of Naboth's vineyard (1 Kings 21). In this story we read of a man who is petty and inadequate—one who must be prodded by his even more wicked wife to get the land that he desires. At the end of the chapter he listens to the judgment of Elijah and repents, and the judgment is mollified. But only in this chapter does the figure of Ahab have depth.

In chapter 22 Ahab is presented again as consistently evil. He must be urged by Jehoshaphat to seek a holy-war oracle. He must be compelled a second time to seek a legitimate Yahweh prophet to do it. His attitude toward the Yahweh prophet is bad from the beginning, and he concludes by ignoring his oracle. He asks for the truth from the prophet, receives it, and then ignores the message. He even has recounted before him the prophet's report of events in the divine council and rejects it. He has the prophet cast into prison. He tries to falsify the oracle by disguising Jehoshaphat in his royal robes and entering battle dressed as a regular warrior.

One of the interesting aspects of the presentation of Ahab in chapter 22 is that he is nowhere named. Some critical scholars have argued on this basis that the narrative (or part of it) may have originally been about a different king.[4] That view misses the point. As Berlin argues, the narrator's attitude toward a character is frequently highlighted by the way he names the characters.[5] It is noticeable that Ahab, who is clearly the focus of concern in this narrative, is never mentioned by name but is always referred to as "the king of Israel." Jehoshaphat is named frequently, but never Ahab. This omission is all the more peculiar because it is clear in this context who he is.

We unfortunately cannot be dogmatic in interpreting the significance of the omission of Ahab's name from the text. It is possible that the narrator felt such disgust that he could not bring himself to name Ahab. On the other hand, the narrator may be emphasizing Ahab's position as "king of Israel" to highlight his culpability. The king should have acted as covenant mediator, but he actually perverted the covenant relationship.

In Chronicles the dramatic difference is that Ahab is a new character introduced for the first time in the narrative. His role, of course, concludes with his death at the end of the story. The

---

[4] DeVries, *I Kings*, pp. 265ff.

[5] Berlin, *Poetics and Interpretation*, pp. 87–91.

interest of this narrative centers on Jehoshaphat. The focus of the camera has shifted to Jehoshaphat, and Ahab is mentioned only because of his connection with Jehoshaphat. Notice also that in Chronicles Ahab *is* identified by name, but only at the beginning in a section significantly modified from the account in 1 Kings.

In conclusion, Ahab, in the Micaiah story in particular and even in the entire section concerning his reign (1 Kings 16:29—22:40), is not a well-rounded figure. The narrator does not expose Ahab's thoughts or feelings. We also lack explanation for his behavior, since the narrative is generally silent concerning motivation. He usually disobeys the prophets, but when he occasionally obeys them, we hear no explanation for his change of heart from the narrator. His character may be summarized by stating simply that he is evil.

Jehoshaphat. Character is often displayed through contrast.[6] We get a partial contrast between Ahab and Jehoshaphat in Kings and in Chronicles. I begin with an analysis of Jehoshaphat's role in the Kings story, though we should note that the Chronicles version is more interested in Jehoshaphat. The contrast with Ahab is found initially in Jehoshaphat's persistent request that a Yahweh prophet be consulted before engaging in battle with the Arameans. Ahab is content with his four hundred court prophets, but Jehoshaphat urges him to bring Micaiah onto the scene. Jehoshaphat appears concerned to seek the will of Yahweh, in spite of Ahab's disinterest.

Even in Kings, however, the contrast between the two kings is not absolute. The second verse indicates that Jehoshaphat went down to Ahab without any mention of a summons. Perhaps there was a summons, but the narrator chose not to mention it and, accordingly, leaves the impression that the initiative was on Jehoshaphat's part. Second, when Ahab asks Jehoshaphat to support him against Ramoth Gilead, the latter's response is immediately affirmative. Only afterward does Jehoshaphat request a holy-war inquiry. Furthermore, after

---

[6] Alter, *The Art of Biblical Narrative,* pp. 72–74, discusses this feature, in reference particularly to dialogue.

Jehoshaphat hears his requested Yahweh oracle, his response is quite surprising. He simply ignores it and goes to battle with Ahab.

The narrator provides no motivation for Jehoshaphat's actions. The lack of explicit motivation (which is one form of gapping) is typical of Old Testament narrative. The reader is left to infer the motivations. In the light of the oracle and its historical outcome, it is clear that the narrator views Jehoshaphat in a negative light.

In Chronicles this negative assessment of Jehoshaphat's actions increases dramatically. Whereas in Kings Jehoshaphat is introduced for the first time in connection with Ahab, in Chronicles he has been brought on the scene a chapter earlier. Second Chronicles 17 shows Jehoshaphat to be faithful in his early years, and as a result of his obedience, God blesses him with prosperity, which results in honor and wealth.

Jehoshaphat's wealth and honor are reemphasized at the beginning of the Micaiah story (2 Chron. 18:1a), followed by the statement that Jehoshaphat was related to Ahab by marriage and treaty. The effect of mentioning Jehoshaphat's wealth immediately before his treaty with the northern kingdom is significant. God granted Jehoshaphat wealth; he did not need a treaty with Ahab! Seen in this light, the conjunction (*waw*) that unites the two sentences of 18:1 should be translated "but" and not "and." The reference to Jehoshaphat's unnecessary treaty alliance at the beginning of the narrative shapes the reader's attitude against Jehoshaphat.

Furthermore, the reshaped introduction to the Micaiah story presents Jehoshaphat as an equal or near-equal with Ahab, which heightens the Judean king's culpability. When Jehoshaphat first arrives, the Chronicles narrator informs the reader about the royal reception he receives. In short, Ahab wines and dines Jehoshaphat, presumably with the intention of persuading (not commanding) him to enter the war as his ally.

This interpretation of the Chronicler's modified introduction is confirmed by his changed conclusion. The report of an encounter between Jehoshaphat and Jehu ben Hanani (2 Chron. 19:1–3) replaces the evaluation of the death of Ahab by the

King's narrator. Jehu explicitly condemns Jehoshaphat's treaty connections with Ahab.

Micaiah. The narrator never comments on Micaiah. He is presented exclusively through dialogue. Ahab's speech represents one perspective or point of view. The narrator places Micaiah in a good light by showing Ahab speaking badly of him. Ahab selects him immediately as a true prophet, the kind that Jehoshaphat wants, but he also maligns him.

The narrator gives Micaiah more depth than the other characters, which is shown in his speech before Ahab. When the messenger counsels Micaiah to conform his oracle to that of the other four hundred prophets, Micaiah rejects his suggestions immediately, saying that he must speak the word of God. Surprisingly, his initial speech before Ahab affirms Ahab's battle plans. The context makes it clear, however, that Micaiah spoke with ironic intent (see the discussion of irony in chapter 4), something Ahab realized without hesitation. When commanded to tell the truth, Micaiah delivers a judgment oracle. The effect of the irony is to heap more blame on Ahab. The initial, ironic prophecy evokes a command from Ahab to "tell the truth." When Ahab hears the truth, he recognizes it as such but blatantly rejects it.

Alter has commented on the narrator's ability to shape character by contrast, often by contrast in speech style and length. The only lengthy, smooth speech in the whole narrative is delivered by Micaiah as he gives God's sentence of judgment. This speech contrasts with all of the short, choppy speeches elsewhere in the story.

In the contrast drawn between Micaiah and Zedekiah and between Micaiah and Ahab, it is noteworthy to observe who has the last word. In both cases, Micaiah points to the future sure fulfillment of his prophetic word (I Kings 22:25, 28). Nonetheless, there is no real interest in Micaiah as a developed character. For one thing, we do not learn of his fate. We are left with the strong impression that he was released after the oracle came true, but it is not reported because the narrator felt that it was unimportant.

Agents in the Micaiah narrative. Most of the other characters in the story are agents. They are given no character traits to speak of and are important only for the progress of the plot. Ahab's officials (1 Kings 22:3), his messenger (v. 13), the four hundred (v. 6), the king of Aram and his thirty-two chariot commanders (v. 31), and, most significantly, the anonymous archer (v. 34) are among those in this category.

ACTS 10:1–11:18: THE GENTILES COME INTO THE CHURCH

My New Testament example of prose analysis also comes from a book that has received less treatment from a literary perspective than other narrative portions. Most attention has been given to the Gospels, while Acts and Revelation, the other two major works of prose in the New Testament, have been relatively ignored. The epistles of the New Testament involve a whole different set of literary questions.[7]

Plot and Setting

The story in Acts 10:1–11:18 centers on the conversion of Cornelius, his relatives, and close friends. The broader story continues at least until Acts 15, when the implications of Gentile inclusion in the church and specifically Paul's ministry to the Gentiles is dealt with, but our attention will be restricted initially to a consideration of the story surrounding the conversion of Cornelius.

The shape of the plot is somewhat different from what we observed in the Micaiah story. Here we have a story with four episodes and two narrative climaxes. The four episodes are distinguished by a shift in setting. For the most part the *fabula* and the *sjužet* (see "Plot" in chapter 4) are the same. That is, the story is told in a fairly straightforward manner, which parallels

---

[7] N. R. Petersen raises two methodological points in his book *Rediscovering Paul: Philemon and the Sociology of Paul's Narrative World* (Philadelphia: Fortress, 1985). He demonstrates that Paul's letters are amenable to a literary approach, since behind the letters are stories. Second, he shows how a literary analysis intersects with a sociological analysis.

the way in which Peter later narrates these amazing events to his brethren in Jerusalem ("Peter began and explained everything to them precisely as it had happened" [Acts 11:4]).

The first episode (10:1–8) is located in Caesarea in the home of a certain Gentile named Cornelius. The story opens by describing Cornelius as a Gentile and as "devout and God-fearing." The opening incident involves a vision that comes to Cornelius while he is in prayer. An angel, whom Cornelius addresses as "Lord," appears before him and instructs him to send for Peter, who is in Joppa.

The second episode (10:9–23a) shifts to Joppa and to Peter. There is also a time shift, since the introduction to this episode mentions that it is already the next day and the messengers who have been sent by Cornelius are nearing their destination. Peter too receives a vision. The vision confuses him because it strikes at the heart of his previous conceptions of how God relates to men and women. The vision is repeated three times, and each time Peter is exhorted to eat unclean food that is lowered from heaven in a sheet. As Peter attempts to understand the meaning of the vision, he is approached by the three men, who ask Peter to go to Caesarea with them. Peter takes the first step of faith and allows the three men to stay in his house as his guests.

The third episode (10:23b–48) shifts the setting back to the house of Cornelius. Peter significantly moves from his own Jewish household into a Gentile household, an act that goes against his previous conception of what God expected of him (vv. 28–29).

In this third episode the visions of the first two are brought together and the result is further clarification of the will of God. Cornelius narrates to Peter (our first instance of narrative flashback and repetition) the message that he had received from God four days earlier. Cornelius realizes that God has brought Peter to him for a purpose, and he stands ready to hear what Peter has to say on behalf of the Lord.

At this point the implications of the vision become clear to Peter, and he delivers the longest speech in the narrative, asserting that God accepts the Gentiles. As he speaks, Cornelius and his party manifest the gifts of the Spirit, and Peter and the other Jewish believers who were with him feel compelled to baptize them.

The first major portion of the plot surrounds the conversion of Cornelius and his household and centers on a conflict. The conflict is between Peter's theological prejudice and God's intention to include the Gentiles. The occasioning incident of the plot, then, is first of all the vision to Cornelius, but even more clearly Peter's vision, which raises a conflict in his mind that cries out for resolution. The climax of the story comes in Peter's moment of recognition that the Gentiles are recipients of the promise.

The story does not conclude here, however. Peter's personal conflict has found resolution, but now the conflict takes on a broader complexion as the rest of the church hears about this event. Peter goes to Jerusalem to explain himself in the fourth episode of the story (11:1–18). The conflict is now between Peter and the leaders of the church in Jerusalem. The occasioning incident comes when Peter is charged, "You went into the house of uncircumcised men and ate with them" (v. 3).

Peter then responds by narrating the story of his vision. The importance of the vision is highlighted by its being narrated in full a second time (11:5–10). He also recounts the vision of Cornelius, with a notable addition. The apostle reports that God told Cornelius that Peter "will bring you a message through which you and all your household will be saved" (v. 14). After Peter fully explained his actions, the leaders were satisfied and believed that God had indeed given the promise of salvation to the Gentiles. The plot thus again finds an ending in resolution of conflict.

The plot, which as we have argued has an independent unity, is significantly framed by other stories. Peter had been the main focus of Acts until chapter 8, when Saul/Paul is introduced. Paul, of course, is the main character of the rest of the book. The Paul narrative, however, is interrupted briefly with a second Peter narrative that begins in 9:32 and narrates two miracles that Peter performed. Clearly one of Luke's purposes in narrating these miracles before the Cornelius incident is to heighten our confidence in Peter's ministry. The story that immediately follows the Cornelius story also serves to validate the ministry of Peter to Cornelius as it describes the conversion of more Gentiles, a happening that is endorsed by Barnabas, an emissary from the Jerusalem church (11:19–30).

Even more broadly, the story of Peter and Cornelius fits very significantly into the story of the Book of Acts. One of the major functions of that story is to validate Paul's ministry to the Gentiles. As W. R. Long observes, "It is of extreme importance for Luke to show that it was through the ritually sensitive, law abiding Peter that the command to evangelize a Gentile came."[8]

The story takes place over time in three locales. Cornelius is in Caesarea, at this time the capital of Palestine. Significantly, the city is predominantly Gentile. It is a likely place for a Roman centurion to reside. Joppa, being a seaport, was likely a somewhat cosmopolitan town, but the Jewish population there was large. It is significant that Peter went to Cornelius in Caesarea rather than the latter's traveling to Joppa. That Peter was willing to make the trip shows that God was already breaking down the barriers between Jews and Gentiles in Christ (cf. 10:28). The third locale in the Cornelius narrative is Jerusalem. Peter goes there as the conversion of Cornelius moves from a matter of private conscience to that of the entire church. It is expected that Jerusalem be the locale of such a major institutional issue, for in both Luke and Acts "Jerusalem clearly emerges as the geographical locus of authority."[9]

Genre

As with the Micaiah narrative, it is impossible to give a full discussion of the genre of Acts 10:1–11:18 in the brief

---

[8] W. R. Long, "The Trial of Paul in the Book of Acts: Historical, Literary, and Theological Considerations" (Ph.D. diss., Brown University, 1982), p. 293; see also D. P. Moessner, " 'The Christ Must Suffer': New Light on the Jesus—Peter, Stephen, Paul Parallels in Luke-Acts," *NTS* 28 (1986): 220–56.

[9] E. S. Nelson, "Paul's First Missionary Journey as Paradigm: A Literary-Critical Assessment of Acts 13–14" (Ph.D. diss., Boston University, 1982), p. 72.

compass of this chapter. It is an issue of considerable debate, and also, with our understanding of the fluid nature of genre, we know that it is not simply a matter of identifying a single, right genre.

The issue of the genre of this story is, of course, related to or even the same as the question of the genre of Acts as a whole. The debate usually concerns whether Acts is history or romance (or, better, historical fiction). One could conceivably point to certain indications within the text to argue in favor of the author's historical intention. I have in mind such things as details concerning characters that are of no special relevance to the plot. For instance, the narrator informs the reader that Peter was staying with Simon in Joppa but adds the fact that Simon was a tanner and that his house was by the sea. Cornelius is identified as an officer in the Italian Regiment. Furthermore, the narrative is given a close chronology. The time of day of Cornelius's prayer is given (10:3), as is the time of Peter's prayer (v. 9).

These incidental details in the story certainly give the impression that the author is concerned to impart historical information. Of course, a skeptic could point out that historical fiction also has such realism effects. However, remembering that the subject of the story is of decided importance for the practice of the early church in that it is citing a precedent for the inclusion of the Gentiles into the church, we see that the author clearly intends his reader to believe that the story took place in history.

Nonetheless, as with Old Testament historiography, it would be a disservice to the text to identify the genre as mere history. Once again we have *didactic* or *theological history*. Perhaps even better, since I am persuaded that Acts serves to justify Paul's ministry to the Gentiles, *apologetic history*.

Characterization

In our discussion of plot we have already touched on the characters. My summary here will accordingly be brief.

Cornelius. The introduction of Cornelius marks the beginning of the narrative. The narrator provides a description of him that, by virtue of its length alone, signals that he is an important character. He is initially presented with an emphasis on the fact that he is a Gentile. His name is a good Roman name. He is a centurion in the Roman army and lives in a predominantly Gentile city. The other emphasis that the narrator relates to the reader is that Cornelius is a kindhearted and religious man (10:2). The narrator's assessment of the centurion's personality is confirmed later by his messengers (v. 22).

Here is a man, then, who clearly is non-Jewish but religious. His heart is in the right place, but he is also somewhat confused. The latter point is illustrated when he first encounters Peter, and he does not know the proper way to relate to him (10:26). God is about to set him straight.

Peter. The other major figure in the story is of course Peter, and as so often happens in biblical texts, there is a contrast. Whereas Cornelius is clearly a Gentile, Peter is obviously a Jew. He is fastidious about Jewish customs, including the provisions that the Jew should stay separate from Gentiles and that they should not eat certain foods. It has long been recognized that these two customs are related. That is, the division between clean and unclean foods represents a similar division in humankind between the clean (Jew) and the unclean (Gentile).

Peter was consistent in his practice of such Jewish customs, which is heightened in the narrative by the fact that God must three times repeat the vision of the sheet lowering from heaven. Even after the vision, Peter has not understood what God has said. Peter's slowness in responding to the revelation of God also provides a contrast with Cornelius, who earlier had immediately responded to God's instruction.

Minor characters. Only one other character is named in the narrative—Simon the tanner. His significance has been mentioned above as injecting an atmosphere of realism into the narrative. Perhaps too his occupation is cited because tanning implies work with dead animals, which would lead to ritual uncleanness. Of even greater importance to the story, however, are four different groups.

The first group is *Cornelius's messengers*. One might ask why they were necessary; God could have told Peter to go to Cornelius's house through his vision. However, the nature of the vision went against everything Peter had previously believed, and the messengers function as a kind of external confirmation of what God had spoken through the vision. Then, we have *Peter's associates*. The text mentions six men who accompanied Peter to Cornelius's house (10:23; 11:12). They serve as witnesses on Peter's behalf to the work that God performed, for they too observed the work of the Holy Spirit. Third, *Cornelius's family and friends* were also saved (10:24, 44). Cornelius was not just an anomaly. Finally, the *apostles and brothers in Jerusalem* criticize and then affirm Peter's actions with Cornelius. Their role emphasizes the fact that Peter is not acting autonomously but that the inclusion of the Gentiles has the approval of the heart of the institutional church.

The Lord/the angel/the Spirit. Of course, the real mover of the narrative is God Himself. He is the one who appears to Cornelius and to Peter and effectively brings them together. The Spirit too is the one who saved the Gentiles and demonstrated to the Jewish believers that Gentiles were also included.

Narrator and Point of View

Once again, this subject interlocks with our previous discussion. Plot, characterization, and the point of view of the narrator are all dependent on one another. The type of third-person narration that we observe in the Cornelius story has already been discussed in conjunction with the Micaiah narrative. Such third-person omniscient narration is the norm in biblical storytelling.

The Cornelius story is narrated in full by an unnamed, omniscient, omnipresent narrator. Through his portrayal of the people and events involved in this story, he guides our reaction and forms our evaluation of it. He makes us, as readers, react positively to Cornelius. We also struggle with Peter and recognize that the inclusion of Cornelius into the household of faith was not an easy decision for Peter to make. We also learn through the narrator that Peter's decision was not quickly accepted by the church authorities in Jerusalem. All in all, we are thereby led to conclude that the right, and not the easy, decision has been made. God has indeed acted to bring the Gentiles into the church. To deny this conclusion is to deny God Himself.

6

THE ANALYSIS OF
POETIC PASSAGES

A surprising amount of the Bible is poetic. Poetry is primarily found in the Old Testament, though there are occasional poetic portions in the New Testament (e.g., Phil. 2:6–11). Within the Old Testament, poetic verse is concentrated in the Psalms and the so-called wisdom books (Song of Songs, Ecclesiastes, Proverbs, and Job). We must not forget, though, that the prophets also wrote energetic verse. Indeed, poetry is the predominant style of the prophets. Ancient poems are encountered in the Pentateuch (Gen. 49; Exod. 15; Deut. 32–33) as well as the historical books (Judg. 5; 2 Sam. 22). Poetry makes up about one-third of the whole Bible and would alone constitute a book the size of the whole New Testament.

Since the conventions that are associated with biblical poetry are foreign to us, poetry presents a number of questions to the modern reader. The poetry of the Bible is unlike its prose and also unlike modern poetry. We must therefore inquire into the workings of poetry in order to guide our reading of the biblical text.

Many exciting insights have been gained recently toward the understanding of biblical poetry. J. Kugel, followed by R. Alter, has modified our approach to semantic parallelism.[1] A.

---

[1] Kugel, *The Idea of Biblical Poetry*; R. Alter, *The Art of Biblical Poetry* (New York: Basic Books, 1985).

Berlin has recently carried the discussion into the area of grammatical parallelism, and M. O'Connor's learned tome anticipated this interest in the nonsemantic aspects of parallelism.[2] The workings of imagery, particularly metaphor, have received much attention in both secular and biblical interpretation.[3] A new consensus on meter is merging, which, though negative, serves to move research beyond an impasse that has hindered our understanding of Hebrew poetry for centuries.[4]

DEFINITION OF POETRY

In the past, poetry has been distinguished from prose in the Bible by the presence of one or more key traits. Parallelism often has been cited as the poetic device *par excellence*. Many poems, however, demonstrate weak or even no parallelism, while parallelism is found in prose portions of Scripture as well. Meter also has been taken as a defining characteristic of poetry, on analogy with classical and most English poetic traditions. Nonetheless, no system of meter has been definitively uncovered in the Bible.

These facts have led Kugel to reject the presence of poetry in the Bible.[5] This position is overstated, however, because the difference between prose and poetry in the Bible is gradated or fluid, which is to be expected, since all generic distinctions are fluid and not absolute or rigid.

Poetry may be defined over against prose by reference to ordinary speech. Prose represents a certain departure from normal speech patterns and poetry a further departure. Poetry is

---

[2] A. Berlin, *The Dynamics of Biblical Parallelism* (Bloomington: Indiana University Press, 1985); M. O'Connor, *Hebrew Verse Structure* (Winona Lake, Ind.: Eisenbrauns, 1980).

[3] G. B. Caird, *The Language and Imagery of the Bible* (Philadelphia: Westminster, 1980); P. Ricoeur, *The Rule of Metaphor* (Toronto: University of Toronto Press, 1977); T. Hawkes, *Metaphor* (London: Methuen, 1972); Sheldon Sacks, ed., *On Metaphor* (Chicago: University of Chicago Press, 1978); M. Black, *Models and Metaphors* (Ithaca: Cornell University Press, 1962).

[4] T. Longman, III, "A Critique of Two Recent Metrical Systems." *Bib* 63 (1982): 230–54.

[5] Kugel, *The Idea of Biblical Poetry*, pp. 59–95.

a more self-consciously structured language. It is self-referring in the sense that increased attention is given to how something is said as well as to what is said. In this manner, poetry is characterized by a higher level of literary artifice than prose. Poetry may best be defined, then, through a description of the various conventions or devices encountered in the poems themselves. Prose is the relative absence of these devices. Instead of characterizing prose and poetry as discrete literary forms, we may better represent them as poles on a continuum, as in the following diagram:

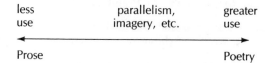

| less use | parallelism, imagery, etc. | greater use |

Prose — Poetry

The rest of this chapter will be devoted to an exposition of the major literary conventions that cluster in Hebrew poetry: terseness, parallelism, and imagery. Space does not permit explanation of occasional poetic devices, for which I refer the reader to W. G. E. Watson's excellent handbook.[6]

PRIMARY FEATURES OF POETRY

Terseness

The most neglected feature of Hebrew poetry is also one of its most common and distinctive traits: the lines of Hebrew poetry are terse; they are short and to the point. By comparison, lines are much longer in prose, which one can easily see by opening a typical English translation of the Old Testament to a poetic passage and looking at the layout of the poem on the page. Poetry is easily recognized because the lines are short.

Prose passages are composed of sentences that are grouped into paragraphs. Poetic passages, on the other hand, may be

---

[6] W. G. E. Watson, *Classical Hebrew Poetry* (*JSOT* 26; Sheffield: JSOT, 1984). For a more popular treatment, see my *How to Read the Psalms* (Downers Grove, Ill.: InterVarsity, forthcoming).

analyzed as consisting of clauses (or cola) that often are bound together into lines by semantic or grammatical repetition. Two cola so bound are labeled a bicolon; three, a tricolon; and so forth. Furthermore, the sentences of a prose passage vary in terms of length. Cola of poetic passages tend to be equal in length.

A device that intensifies the terseness of the poetic line in Hebrew is *ellipsis*. Frequently a noun but more commonly a verb occurs in the first colon of a line but has no parallel in the second colon. The verb in the first colon is understood in the second colon, for instance, in Psalm 33:12:

> Blessed is the nation whose God is the LORD,
>   the people he chose for his inheritance.

The opening word *blessed* is missing from the second colon, but to make sense of the line we must supply the word. Such ellipsis is quite common in biblical poetry.

A further aspect of the terseness of biblical verse is the lack of conjunctions and particles. The conjunctions *and, but, or* and the temporal markers *then, when, afterward* are rare in poetry. Logical markers such as *therefore* and *thus,* as well as the causal marker *because* occur infrequently. Since conjunctions function to guide the reader in his or her interpretation of the temporal or logical relationships between statements, their lack introduces an element of intentional ambiguity into the text.

Parallelism

While terseness is usually omitted in studies of Hebrew poetry, parallelism is often identified as the single major poetic device. Indeed, parallelism for all practical purposes frequently is equated with poetry. J. Kugel, however, has shown the fallacy of taking parallelism as the key to the definition of poetry.[7] On the one hand, he shows that many poems have either no parallelism or a very weak form of it. The first few

---

[7] Kugel, *The Idea of Biblical Poetry.*

lines of Jeremiah's complaint in chapter 12 show little parallelism except in the last two cola:

> You are always righteous, O LORD,
>   when I bring a case before you.
> Yet I would speak with you about your justice:
>   Why does the way of the wicked prosper?
>   Why do all the faithless live at ease?

Furthermore, it has long been recognized that prose passages often show a symmetry that can be described as parallelistic. Kugel provides the following example from Genesis 21:1:

> And the LORD remembered Sarah as he had said
>   and the LORD did for Sarah as he had spoken.[8]

Nonetheless, parallelism, while not the defining characteristic of poetry, is certainly one of its major ornamental devices. Repetition abounds within lines (internal parallelism) and between the lines (external parallelism) of a typical Old Testament poem. The parallelism operates on both semantic and grammatical levels.

Semantic Parallelism. Jeremiah 30:12–14 provides clear examples of semantic parallelism in Hebrew poetry:

> "Your wound is incurable,
>   your injury beyond healing.
> There is no one to plead your cause,
>   no remedy for your sore,
>   no healing for you.
> All your allies have forgotten you;
>   they care nothing for you."

In the first two cola, "wound" and "injury" are close in meaning, as are "incurable" and "beyond healing." These parallel words lead the reader to meditate on one colon in the light of the other. In other words, repetition exhibits the coherence between two cola.

The obvious repetition that appears between cola in a parallel line has led to an overevaluation of the similarity between the lines. As a result, parallelism has even been

---

[8] Ibid., p. 59.

described as two cola that express the same meaning twice, using two different sets of words. Such a definition of parallelism is extremely misleading, for it causes the reader to gloss over the progression from one colon to another. While cola show similarity with one another, there are also intentional divergences, differences of meaning to which attention must be given.

Once again, Kugel has been the scholar who has brought this important point to light. In traditional approaches to parallelism the first colon (A) of a parallel line is *equal* in meaning to the second colon (B).[9] Kugel, on the other hand, argues that the thought of the second colon always progresses in some way beyond the first, in his formulation, "A—what's more, B."

The beginning of Psalm 72 contains two parallel lines that are bicola:

> Endow the king with your justice, O God,
>   the royal son with your righteousness.
> He will judge your people in righteousness,
>   your afflicted ones with justice.

We may observe both similarity and difference between the cola in these lines. The imperative verb "endow" is elided from the second colon of the first line but is understood there. The object of the verb is "king" in the first colon but is expanded in the second as "royal son." There is some ambiguity between two interpretations of "son," but in either case the second colon progresses beyond the thought of the first. Either the royal son is equated with the king (that is, he is God's son [see 2 Sam. 7:14]), or the phrase refers to the king's son, the heir. In the latter case, the progression of thought is obvious, since it refers to a second individual. In the former reading, the reference

---

[9] The traditional view is based on the work of R. Lowth, who lived in the eighteenth century and whose main insights into the workings of Hebrew poetry are found in his *Sacred Poetry of the Hebrews*. He is also well known for his tripartite division of semantic parallelism into synonymous, antithetic, and synthetic. For a critique of this typology of parallelism, consult Kugel, *The Idea of Biblical Poetry,* and my forthcoming *How to Read the Psalms*.

becomes more personal by highlighting the divine sonship of the king.

Psalm 37 begins with the following two lines:

> Do not fret because of evil men
>   or be envious of those who do wrong;
> for like the grass they will soon wither,
>   like green plants they will soon die away.

Once again we see illustrated the principle that the second colon develops the thought expressed in the first. The similarity between the cola in both of the lines leads the reader to consider them together, to meditate on how they relate, and to note how the second line reinforces the thought of the first.

The first line is brought together most forcefully by the parallel between "evil men" and "those who do wrong." Some progression may be observed in that the latter expression further defines the former. The progression is clearer with the verbs. The psalmist insists that the hearer/reader not worry about the evil men. More specifically, however, the reader is admonished not to be jealous. In this context, "envy" is more specific than "fret." One might fret for a variety of reasons (fear being the most obvious); in the second line, however, envy is singled out.

The second parallel line is grammatically subordinate to the first. Once again the progression is obvious between the verbs. In the first colon, the plants "wither." This thought is intensified in the second colon in that the plants "die."

In summary, semantic parallelism is frequently an ornament of biblical poetry. A verse often combines two similar, yet subtly divergent, cola. The second element of the verse always carries forward the thought of the first.

Grammatical parallelism. Our discussion has centered so far on semantic parallelism, for two reasons: (1) only recently have scholars seriously applied themselves to study grammatical parallelism, and (2) grammatical parallelism is not as directly relevant to the meaning of a poem. I mention grammatical parallelism here because, like semantic parallelism, it is another method writers used to relate cola to each other. The grammatical similarity between two cola in a bicolon will cause the reader to read them closely together, and subtle variations between the cola in terms of syntax add interest to the line. In short, it is another factor that leads us to describe the poetic line as exhibiting both coherence and variance, similarity and dissimilarity, symmetry and asymmetry.

Grammatical parallelism simply describes the relationship between the syntax and morphology of cola in a poetic line. Scholarly analysis of grammatical parallelism can be technical. I discuss here one well-presented view, that of T. Collins, as an example.[10]

Collins's basic premise is borrowed from transformational grammar, which postulates a finite number of basic sentences (deep structure) that generate an infinite number of actual sentences (surface structure). Simply put, Collins describes four basic sentences of Hebrew, defined by the grammatical units that they contain: (1) subject and verb; (2) subject, verb, and modifier; (3) subject, verb, and object; and (4) subject, verb, object, and modifier. The next step in his analysis involves the description and application of four "general line types." These types define the relations of basic sentences to one another: (1) lines that have one basic sentence; (2) lines that occur with two identical basic sentences; (3) lines that contain two similar basic sentences, with the second one only partially repeating the first syntactically; and (4) lines that have two completely different basic sentences.

Contrary to Collins's position, grammatical parallelism is not the key to the definition of poetry. The categories are too loose, and it is hard to imagine any line in the Bible, poetry or prose, as incapable of analysis by them. On the positive side, however, the analysis of the syntactic shape of poetical lines yields a picture of coherence and variation or similarity and dissimilarity that is like what we have in semantic parallelism. A. Berlin has written recently on the grammatical aspect of parallelism from this basic starting point:

---

[10] T. Collins, *Line-Forms in Hebrew Poetry* (Rome: Biblical Institute Press, 1978).

The grammatical aspect of parallelism—grammatical equivalence and/or contrast—is one of the fundamental aspects of biblical parallelism. There is almost always some degree of grammatical correspondence between parallel lines, and in many cases it is the basic structuring device of the parallelism—the feature that creates the perception of parallelism.[11]

One of the differences between prose and poetry is the free variation in syntax of the latter. Frequently, the syntactic shape within a poetic line will be the same but with subtle differences. The similar aspects of the cola in a line have the effect that readers will take the two cola as one unit, but the dissimilarity reminds them that the second colon is not a similar statement but a furtherance or sharpening of the first.[12]

The following is a simple syntactic analysis of Deuteronomy 32:1 (V = verb; S = subject; M = modifier; O = object).

Listen, O heavens, and I will speak;
  V   S   M

hear, O earth, the words of my mouth.
  V   S   O

In this first bicolon we observe a close syntactic parallelism between the first two elements of the cola, but then variation in the third section. Instead of a verb clause (acting as a modifier) in third position, the poet places a direct object in the second colon. Such variation breaks the monotony of repetition and lends interest to the line.

More subtle variations may also be seen in the Hebrew original of this simple bicolon. For instance, there is morphological variation between the verbs in the two cola[13] The first verb is causative (hiphil) and masculine, while the second verb is not causative (qal) and is feminine. Such variations help gain the attention of the Hebrew reader. The line on one level has the potential for being rather monotonous. Both "listen" and

---

[11] Berlin, The Dynamics, p. 31.

[12] The term sharpening was apparently introduced into the description of parallelism by Kugel, The Idea of Biblical Poetry, pp. 11–12.

[13] For the distinction within grammatical parallelism between syntactic and morphological parallelism, consult Berlin, The Dynamics, pp. 32–63.

"hear" and "heaven" and "earth" are frequently occurring word pairs.[14] The subtle variations of syntax and morphology that we just noticed add a level of sophistication to the line.

The next two bicola (Deut. 32:2) show a similar grammatical parallelism (PP = prepositional phrase).

> Let my teaching fall like rain
>   S   V   PP
>
> and my words descend like dew,
>   S   V   PP
>
> like showers on new grass,
>   PP   PP
>
> like abundant rain on tender plants.
>   PP   PP

These two bicola contain more similarities than the line from verse 1. Nonetheless, one may still observe subtle morphological differences. The masculine verb in the first colon, for instance, is answered by a feminine verb in the second.

These two examples of grammatical parallels illustrate lines that are relatively high in similarity. Many lines, particularly from later time periods (eighth century B.C. and after), show much less similarity of structure. Overall, it may be said without hesitation that Hebrew poetry shows more freedom in syntax (word order) than prose. Such freedom allows the subtle variations between cola that we observe. Syntactic variation is thus another element of language play that characterizes Hebrew verse.

Imagery

Imagery occurs in prose as well as in poetry. Since its use is intensified and heightened in poetry, however, and since it is one of the chief characteristics of poetic language, I have reserved discussion until this chapter. A literary image is a

---

[14]For a near-exhaustive study of word pairs, see Y. Avishur, *Stylistic Studies of Word-pairs in Biblical and Ancient Semitic Literature* (Kevelaer: Butzon & Bercker, 1984).

sensation evoked in the mind of the reader by the language of a text. As C. Day Lewis states in an often-quoted definition, "It is a picture made out of words."[15] Or as N. Friedman asserts:

> Imagery refers to images produced in the mind by language, whose words and statements may refer either to experiences which could produce physical perceptions were the reader actually to have those experiences, or to the sense-impressions themselves.[16]

The type of imagery that is our concern is virtually identical with *figurative language*. Unlike literal language, figurative language does not mean what it seems to mean on the surface. We may heartily agree with T. Hawkes when he observes that "all language, by the nature of its 'transferring' relation to 'reality' . . . is fundamentally metaphorical."[17] Perhaps what we call literal language is composed of dead (in the sense of forgotten) metaphors.[18] Nonetheless, a practical distinction may be made between literal and figurative language.

The scope of this book does not permit a detailed listing of the many different kinds of images encountered in literature in general and the Bible in particular. A major division may be suggested between imagery that functions on the basis of association or contiguity and that which functions on the basis of similarity.

Similarity. Images based on similarity are the most common in the Bible. In order to describe a person, object, or event, the poet will explicitly or implicitly compare the item with something or someone else that is similar in some way but that is also different. The difference between the two causes the reader to recognize the presence of an image and stimulates him

---

[15] Quoted in N. Friedman, "Imagery," in the *Princeton Encyclopedia of Poetry and Poetics,* ed. A. Preminger (Princeton: Princeton University Press, 1965), p. 363.

[16] Ibid.

[17] Hawkes, *Metaphor,* p. 60.

[18] G. Lakoff and M. Johnson, *Metaphors We Live By* (Chicago: University of Chicago Press, 1980).

or her to search for the similarity within the difference that the image conceals.

Many different types of image are based on the principle of similarity (personification, allegory, symbol, etc.), but the most common is metaphor, with its explicit correlate, simile. I concentrate here on metaphor. (Indeed it might plausibly be argued that all of the others are really a subtype of the master figure, metaphor.) A metaphor is an image based on similarity within difference. In Song of Songs 2:1, the beloved describes herself: "I am a rose of Sharon, a lily of the valleys." This sentence is absurd if interpreted literally. The differences shock us into realizing that this verse is imagery. The beloved is not describing herself as having one long green leg capped by a red or white head. The reader intuitively and meditatively must consider the similarity between the woman and the flowers by means of a process of elimination. This process will result in some vagueness of interpretation, but vagueness is an inherent characteristic of figurative language. Among the possible intended similarities between the woman in the Song of Songs and the flowers are beauty and pleasant smell.

Students of metaphor have subdivided different types. One of the most productive typologies of metaphor is that presented by G. B. Caird. He explains that metaphor may be broken down into "four points of comparison."[19] The first is *perceptual* metaphor and is based on one of the senses. The most common is visual, but this kind has often been overemphasized to the extent that some wrongly think that all metaphors are to be visualized. For instance, the sense of smell may be the important point of comparison in a metaphor. Psalm 141:2 compares the psalmist's prayer with the sweet smell of incense. Though a simile, Ecclesiastes 7:6 illustrates a comparison based on sound: "Like the crackling of thorns under the pot, so is the laughter of fools." Taste is in the center of the comparison in Song of Songs 7:2: "Your navel is a rounded goblet that never

---

[19] For the definitions and examples considered in this section, see Caird, *Language and Imagery*, pp. 145ff.

lacks blended wine." Of course, metaphors may evoke a plurality of senses.

Caird defines *pragmatic* Lietaphor as a comparison in which "we compare the activity or result of one thing with that of another." Isaiah 10:5 is a good example: "Woe to the Assyrian, the rod of my anger." The rod, which is an instrument of punishment, is compared with Assyria, a nation that God used to punish the rebellious northern kingdom.

The other two types of comparison are less frequent in the Scriptures than the first two. *Synesthetic* comparison may be seen as a subtype of perceptual in that it is "the use in connexion with one of the senses of terms which are proper to another" (Psalm 55:21: "His speech is smooth as butter").

Affective comparisons are "those in which the feel or value, the effect or impression of one thing is compared with that of another." Speaking to the king of Assyria concerning the certain downfall of his nation, Nahum says, "Nothing can heal your wound; your injury is fatal" (Nah. 3:19).

Images of Association. Perhaps the two most well-known figures of speech based on the principle of association as opposed to similarity are *metonymy* and *synecdoche*. The former has been defined as "the substitution of one word for another word closely associated with it."[20] For instance, in Psalm 45:6, God's throne stands for his kingship. Synecdoche, on the other hand, is when a part stands for the whole. For instance, references to God's "right hand" and "holy arm" are synecdochic for God Himself.

The Function of Imagery. Imagery, like poetic language in general, lacks the precision of most literal language. The meaning of a metaphor, we have seen above, is located in the similarity between two things that are also different. The similarity is unstated or hidden, and the reader must meditate on the metaphor to arrive at its interpretation. The result is lack of precision.

Imagery compensates for the lack of precision by its increase in vividness. Images are frequently clear and memor-

---

[20] Ryken, *The Bible as Literature,* p. 101.

able. The simile of God as a drunk waking up from a long slumber (Ps. 78:65) is vivid and hard to forget because it is so striking. Images also speak directly to the heart. They are emotionally charged and often induce us to action of some sort or another. The image of God as shepherd as particularly expressed in Psalm 23 speaks to our heart and will as well as to our minds in a way that is impossible to paraphrase in prose.

Images also serve to bring our attention to old truths in new ways. Technically, this function of imagery and literature in general has been called distanciation or defamiliarization. For instance, the people of Israel may have become calloused to the prophet's message of coming judgment as a result of their sins, so Hosea preaches the old message of judgment through a series of gripping images in 13:3:

> Therefore they will be like the morning mist,
>   like the early dew that disappears,
>   like chaff swirling from a threshing floor,
>   like smoke escaping through a window.

Jesus frequently taught by parables, a type of extended metaphor. He used parables to communicate ethical or theological principles.

Meter

Meter is common in the poetic traditions best known to us. Greek, Roman, English, and American poems, with some exceptions, have metrical structures. The modern student virtually equates poetic expression with meter. Scholars have thus long assumed that Hebrew poetry is metrical. The issue, then, has been not whether biblical poetry is metrical but what kind of meter it displays.

Meter is best defined in relationship to rhythm. Rhythm is the unsystematic alternation of stressed and unstressed syllables. Prose and everyday speech are rhythmical. Meter differs from rhythm by being both regular and predictable. In other words, meter has a pattern. According to the literary critic P. Fussel, "Meter is what results when the natural rhythmical movements of colloquial speech are heightened, organized, and regulated so that pattern—which means repetition—emerges from the relative phonetic haphazard of ordinary utterance."[21]

Fussel also shows how meter generates meaning. Meter is not simply an ornament of language. He distinguishes three functions of meter. First, it triggers a reading strategy. Meter gives language an artificial air that signals to the reader that the text is poetry. Fussel likens the function of meter in literature to that of the picture frame around the painting of a landscape. The frame borders and separates the landscape from reality. Second, meter sets up a regular, repeated pattern. A departure from that pattern thus lends emphasis to the variant word or phrase. Finally, certain metrical patterns are sometimes associated with certain ideas or moods. Fussel cites the limerick as an example of a metrical form that is connected with a light-hearted mood. In biblical texts scholars have attempted to identify a certain metrical form (3-2 in an accentual schema) with laments, the so-called qinah.[22]

With reference to biblical poems, it can be said that, if the metrical pattern of Hebrew poems could be discerned, researchers would have a reliable tool to use in determining the original text of a poem. Indeed, for years scholars have been citing "metrical reasons" for the addition or omission of words and phrases from the poems. The critical apparatus of modern Hebrew texts is littered with the notation *metri causa* to justify textual emendations. Furthermore, if a metrical pattern could be discovered, it would be useful toward the discovery of the structure of the poems.

With all this benefit in discerning meter, it is disappointing to learn that no consensus has been reached on the metrical structure of biblical poetry. A great many systems have been proposed, but not one has won general acceptance. The two most popular approaches to meter are the older accentual meter and the newer syllable-counting meter.

---

[21] P. Fussel, Jr., *Poetic Meter and Poetic Form* (New York: Random House, 1965), p. 5.

[22] See, for example, W. R. Garr, "The Qinah: A Study of Poetic Meter, Syntax, and Style," *ZAW* 95 (1983): 54–74.

The accentual approach to meter highlights the long syllables of words according to Masoretic accents. In the Masoretic accentual system, each word, regardless of its length, receives one stress (except for proclitics joined by the hyphen *maqqef*). In Hebrew the accent is usually on the last syllable. There is, however, great diversity in the way that the various practitioners of accentual meter apply their method. Such differences have to do partly with the use of different ancient traditions of accentuation as well as the subjectivity of assigning accents.

Syllable counting reckons the meter of Hebrew poems in analogy with the metrical systems of the French alexandrine and Japanese poetry.[23] As one reads biblical poetry, one is struck by the near equal length of cola. Often two cola of a line that are in parallel have an equal or very nearly equal number of syllables. Advocates of the syllable-counting approach to meter take this fact as evidence that the number of syllables is associated with the metrical pattern.

While these and other metrical schemas are popular and often encountered in commentaries, the tendency of scholars today is to be skeptical of meter. Some maintain that the changes in the language have been such that we cannot detect the meter; others believe that there is no such thing as meter in Hebrew poetry. There is no certain way to decide whether meter is simply unknowable or nonexistent, but the result for practical exegesis is the same in either case. At this point, meter plays simply no role in the exegesis of Hebrew poetry. Looking primarily at the poetic features of parallelism and imagery, we turn now to consider five specific examples of biblical poetry.

---

[23]The most extensive description of the syllable-counting approach to meter is in D. Stuart, *Studies in Early Hebrew Meter* (Missoula, Mont.: Scholars, 1976).

7

EXAMPLES OF
POETIC ANALYSIS

I have selected parts of five poems for analysis to illustrate the poetic conventions described in chapter 6. The first is from the Torah (Exod. 15:1–5); the second, from wisdom literature (Song of Songs 5:10–16). The third selection is a short section of a psalm (51:3–6), while the fourth is an example of prophetic poetry (Mic. 4:2–5). The last example comes from the New Testament (Luke 1:46–55). These analyses are partial and suggestive. I point out primarily only the main conventions of biblical poetry—grammatical and semantic parallelism and imagery (terseness is self-evident).[1]

EXODUS 15:1–5: THE LORD IS A WARRIOR

Exodus 15 is, by general consent, one of the oldest poems in the Bible. As a hymn that praises the redemptive power of God, it is also one of the most memorable. The historical context of the Song of the Sea, as Exodus 15 is also called, is well known. The Israelites just narrowly escaped an angry Pharaoh and his troops. Moses and the Israelites have witnessed

---

[1] In this chapter, some of the poetic structure does not follow the NIV but has been rearranged to express more clearly the structure of the original text.

God's miraculous intervention, which resulted in their salvation and the judgment of their oppressors.

The poem opens:

> I will sing to the LORD, for he is highly exalted
> He has thrown horse and its rider into the sea.

English translations of these two lines often divide them into four cola in order to keep all of the song's cola roughly even in terms of length. Most of the bicola and tricola in Exodus 15 are indeed of very nearly equal length. Nevertheless there are a few long lines, often the initial line or two of a poem. They set the tone for the remainder of the hymn. Such is the function of the two long lines that begin Exodus 15.

The first clear bicolon follows:

> The Lord is my strength and song;
> He has become my salvation.

The second colon parallels the first colon in that the poet adds "salvation" as a third way in which the Lord relates to him. The sense of the line is that God is x and y to me; in addition, he is also z to me. The B colon sharpens the A colon in a second way as well. B is a climatic statement, explaining that the Lord is my strength and song because He is my salvation.

In the Hebrew, each colon in this line has six syllables. There are fewer words in the second colon, but the longer word for "salvation" replaces the two short words for "strength" and "song."

Equal syllable length is not a rigid rule in biblical poetry, which the next bicolon illustrates:

> He is my God, and I will praise Him.
> My father's God, and I will exalt Him.

In Hebrew, the first colon here has seven syllables, and the second has ten. This line is especially unusual in that the second colon is longer than the first. Nonetheless, the second colon functions normally in that it sharpens and carries forward the meaning of the A colon. The association of these two cola is also clear in their grammatical parallelism. First of all, ellipsis unites the two. A full reading of the B colon would begin, "He is (*zeh*) my father's God. . . ." Second, both cola begin with a noun phrase and an explicit mention of God, followed by a verbal clause. Both of the verbs are imperfect first-person singular with *waw* consecutive and also end with a third-person masculine suffix. These syntactic and morphological similarities bind the cola together and lead the reader to meditate on both cola in relationship with one another. Not only is He my God; He is also my father's God. Not only will I praise Him; I will also exalt Him. Both halves of the second line heighten the thought of the first.

The shortest line in the first five verses is also the most important:

> The Lord is a warrior;
> the Lord is his name.

This line explicitly states what the rest of poem describes and implies: God is a powerful warrior, or man of war. This metaphor informs the whole poem and also reverberates through Scripture from beginning to end. Here the image is stated tersely with a powerful effect upon the reader. God is identified as a warrior by way of praise and in reaction to His great redemptive act at the Red Sea.

The relationship between the two cola is not totally clear. Is it saying, "The Lord is a warrior—you heard right, the Lord"? Or perhaps Moses draws attention to the significance of the name Yahweh as it was explained to him at the burning bush (Exod. 3). "The Lord is a warrior—why are you surprised? He is, after all, the one who said, 'I am who I am.'"

The song then returns to meditate specifically on the great deed of God at the Red Sea. It is interesting that the first colon of this long line is similar in both meaning and syntax to the second opening monocolon (see above):

> He has cast the chariots of Pharaoh and his army into
>   the Red Sea.
> The choicest of his officers are drowned in the Red Sea.

The meaning of these two long cola draw them into one line. Each colon is a similar reflection on a single event but is expressed in two different ways with a resultant progression. The intensification that the second colon provides is achieved primarily through stating the consequence of the action of the first colon. In other words, the chariots and armies of Pharaoh are cast into the sea *with the result* that they drowned.

The closing line of this opening section of the Song of the Sea is also a bicolon:

> The deeps covered them;
> they went down into the depths like a stone.

In a normal prose passage only one of these clauses would be necessary. The addition of the second colon serves to make the thought more vivid, especially since it includes a simile.

We can thus observe many of the conventions of Hebrew parallelism in this short section from a very early poem. I have reserved discussion of imagery to this point. While in some of the other examples in this chapter we encounter a number of local images (see especially the Song of Songs example), here we have a major metaphor that permeates the whole text but is expressed concisely in one line:

> The Lord is a warrior;
> the Lord is His name.

The metaphor is that drawn between God and a soldier. God has just won a great victory over a powerful human army. Moses therefore likens Him to a mighty soldier. The image is best labeled an affective metaphor, since the comparison is between the type of victory that a human soldier or army can provide and the one that God has just won over Egypt. The divine warrior is a pervasive image in the Scriptures. It is explicit from this point in biblical history until the time when Jesus Christ will return to wage war against the powers of evil (Rev. 19:11–21).[2]

---

[2]T. Longman, III, "The Divine Warrior: The New Testament Use of an Old Testament Motif," *WTJ* 44 (1982): 290–307, with relevant bibliography.

SONG OF SONGS 5:10–16: THE BELOVED'S PRAISE TO HER LOVER

The Song of Solomon is a collection of loosely associated psalms extolling human love.[3] A common type of song encountered in the book is the hymn in which the man extols the physical beauty of the woman or vice versa. This particular subgenre of love poem has been labeled the *wasf*,[4] a name derived from a similar literary form in modern Arabic love poetry. The *wasf* is a metaphorical description of the body of the man or the woman that normally begins at the head and works down (4:1–7; 6:4–7; cf. the reverse order in 7:1–9). Of the four occurrences in the Song of Songs, the present example is the only one in which the woman describes the man.

The poem begins with a bicolon that commends the man's overall attractiveness.

> My lover is radiant and ruddy,
> conspicuous among ten thousand.

The first colon calls the lover "radiant" and "ruddy"; the second line further specifies his attributes as uncommon, that is, "conspicuous among ten thousand."[5] In this way, the second colon sharpens the first. In Kugel's terms, "My lover is radiant and ruddy—what's more, he is conspicuous among ten thousand!"

The following lines each describe one part of the man's physical appearance and vividly praise his beauty through a metaphor or a simile. This poem treats ten different parts of the man's body. The first line is a monocolon that compares the lover's head to "purest gold." We have already heard that he is ruddy, so the metaphor probably does not refer to the color of his complexion, say, to his golden tan. The primary point of

---

[3] M. Falk, *Love Lyrics from the Bible: A Translation and Literary Study of the Song of Songs* (Sheffield: Almond, 1982).

[4] M. Pope, *Song of Songs* (Anchor Bible 7C; Garden City, N.Y.: Doubleday, 1977), pp. 55–56.

[5] In the following discussion I am much indebted to the philological work done by Pope in his *Song of Songs*, pp. 531–50.

contact is found in the high value of "pure gold." In other words, she prizes her lover above all else.

The second line is a bicolon that focuses on one aspect of the man's head, namely, his hair. "His hair is luxuriant," the woman lovingly says; even more (second colon), it is "black as a raven." The second colon thus adds a further loving description of the man's hair. The first line is literal language; the second is figurative, highlighting the deep blackness of the man's hair. The movement from literal to figurative is a pattern that Alter has noted as being common in biblical poetry.[6]

The next verse (v. 12) is a complex line that describes the man's eyes. The longer first line makes the parallelism unbalanced, and the metaphor is mixed.

> His eyes are like doves by the water streams,
> washed in milk,
> mounted like jewels.

Translations will often break the first colon into two to preserve a similar colon length. There are no substantive poetic reasons for the break, however, only the presumption that all lines must by definition be of near-equal length. We have seen this tendency in Hebrew poetry, but it is not a hard-and-fast rule.

The first colon gives an initial description of the man's eyes, followed by cola that give two further specifications. We need to be especially sensitive to cultural differences as we interpret the meaning of metaphors and other comparisons, including the images in these songs praising physical beauty. Cultures differ in their perception of what makes a body beautiful. Also, metaphorical expressions of that beauty change through time and from culture to culture. In Song of Songs 4:4, for instance, the woman's neck is likened to "the tower of David." Such a compliment would be greeted with contempt by most modern women, even if David's tower were culturally contextualized to a modern equivalent (e.g., the Empire State Building).

The water streams of the simile refer to the moistness of the eyes as does the participle "washed" that begins the second

---

[6] Alter, *The Art of Biblical Poetry*, p. 21.

colon. The point of comparison between doves and eyes is a little difficult, though not unique (see 4:1). Some scholars argue—improbably, I believe—that the man's eyes are compared with the eyes of the dove. Perhaps the delicateness of this bird, or more likely its color, is the point of the comparison. The pupils are likened to the sparkle and preciousness of jewels in the third colon, while in the second the poet captures the whiteness of the eyes with the reference to milk. One is tempted to carry the thought further by saying that the purity of milk suggests the additional dimension of purity or sincerity of character. As modern interpreters, however, we do not know whether milk carried that connotation at the time the Song of Songs was written.

While the previous parallel lines have been grounded on visual comparisons, the next two (v. 13) primarily appeal to the sense of smell. Both cheeks and lips are likened to highly fragrant substances.

The following three lines (vv. 14–15a) drop below the head and deal with the man's limbs and torso (arms, loins, and legs). Here the parallelism is again additive in the sense that the first colon provides one point of description, and the second adds a further specific description. The comparison is once again perceptual, in these cases both visual and tactile. The man's body is compared with beautiful, precious, and hardened substances.

The poem concludes (vv. 15b–16) with a second general description of the lover's overall appearance, followed by a description of his mouth. The mouth comes last in the description, an effective sequence since the woman obviously desires to kiss the man. The point of comparison is appropriately grounded in the sense of taste. His mouth is sweetness itself.

The semantic parallelism is supported by grammatical parallelism. There is both unity and diversity between the lines. In this text the basically similar syntactic pattern between the poetic lines is particularly striking. The first line invariably begins with a noun and suffix. After the initial first-person pronominal suffix on "my love" (v. 10), the pronoun is always "his." After the body part is named, it is then characterized by a noun phrase. The second colon of each of the lines begins with a participle. The participial clause is then completed by either a direct object or a prepositional phrase. Nonetheless, it is astounding that ten participial clauses are found in this short section. The only exceptions are the two monocola (vv. 11a and 16a) that lack any second colon and the description of the eyes (v. 12), which has two participial phrases.

The effect of such syntactic repetition might be monotonous, except that there is a significant amount of morphological variation. Considering only the participles that are the focus of repetition in the passage, we may observe variation between different types of participles including *qal* passive participles (vv. 10b, 16b), *qal* active participles that are feminine plural (vv. 11b, 12b, 12c, 13c), *pual* participles (vv. 14a, 14b, 15a), and a *piel* participle (v. 13b).

PSALM 51:3–6: A CONFESSION OF SIN

Psalm 51 is one of the best-known psalms in the Bible. Modern readers readily identify with its profound confession of sin and its appeal to God for forgiveness. The historical title situates the origin of the poem in the life of David, specifically after he is confronted by Nathan about his sin with Bathsheba (2 Sam. 12). The psalm surely played an important role in the life of the formal worship of God beyond this historical setting—and still does.

Formally, the psalm as a whole may be identified as a lament. Such psalms frequently begin with an invocation to the Lord and an appeal to Him for help. Laments may be subdivided further into those that contain a confession of sin and those that have a proclamation of innocence.[7] Psalm 51 fits into the former category. I have chosen the section containing the psalmist's confession of sin as an example of psalmic poetry. The section begins:

---

[7] See E. Gerstenberger, "Psalms," in *Old Testament Form Criticism* (San Antonio: Trinity University Press, 1974), p. 206.

> For my transgressions I know;
> and my sin is before me continually.

The parallelism between the two cola is firmly based on the common word pair "transgressions" and "sin." Variation occurs in the remainder of the cola. In colon A the psalmist admits awareness of his fault; in colon B, this thought is heightened by adding the temporal dimension. He is aware of his fault *all the time*.

In the next bicolon the psalmist shows that he is aware not only of his sin but of the fact that his sin is an affront to God Himself:

> Against you, you only, I have sinned;
> that which is evil in your eyes I have done.

I have preserved the word order of the Hebrew in order to demonstrate the fact that poetic syntax is often quite different from the norm (which is defined according to the regular word order of prose). In the second colon the word order is direct object, prepositional phrase, and verb. This sequence is quite convoluted over against the typical prose pattern of verb, direct object, and prepositional phrase.

In the next poetic line the two verbs and the two prepositional phrases are clearly parallel to one another, even to the extent that both verbs are *qal,* imperfect, second-person singular.

> So that you are righteous in your ways;
> you are pure in your judgments.

In addition, both of the prepositional phrases begin with the preposition b^e. The intensification, however, that takes place between the two cola is that of a general statement leading to a specific one. Colon A asserts that the Lord is totally righteous in all that He does (the sense of the metaphor "way"), while the second colon focuses on God's judgments and declares that they are "pure."

Turning back to an assessment of himself, the psalmist confesses:

> Indeed in sin I was brought to birth;
> and in sin my mother conceived me.

The verse clearly indicates that the psalmist knows that he has been a sinner since his very beginning. The progress of meaning between the two cola is impossible to miss here. He admits to being a sinner at the time of his birth, and then he goes further in the second colon by confessing that his association with sin extends to the time of his conception.

He concludes:

> Indeed truth you desire in the dark places;
> and in the secret places you teach me wisdom.

Once again there is an obvious parallelism between the cola, with an additional binding by ending the first colon with a prepositional phrase that is both grammatically and semantically parallel with the opening prepositional phrase in colon B. The clearest progression may be seen in the verbs: in the first colon we have the desire of God stated, while in the second we learn that He is the one who teaches wisdom.

MICAH 4:2–5: THE FUTURE GLORY OF ZION

I have chosen a salvation oracle from Micah 4 as an example of prophetic poetry. A study of the whole oracle would require an analysis of the first verse, but I concentrate here on only the four verses that occur after the prose statement "many nations will come and say" (v. 2a).

The Book of Micah is an anthology of oracles that have a definite structure, but it is unnecessary to situate Micah 4 fully before we look at its poetic devices. It is of interest to observe, however, that this oracle that speaks of the future glorification of Zion follows immediately a particularly hard-hitting judgment oracle directed against Zion ("Zion will be plowed like a field" [3:12]).

The parallelism of this oracle is clear, being composed of ten neatly delineated bicola. The repetition in both meaning and grammar causes us to group them into separate bicola, while

the subtle and not-so-subtle variations between the cola of a line
develop the thought.

The opening line is a classic bicolon:

> Come, let us go up to the mountain of the Lord;
> to the God of Jacob's house.

The two lines are bound by ellipsis and by the repetition of the
two prepositional phrases that begin with "to." ('*el*). The
second line advances the meaning of the first by making the
reference more specific. After all, the house of the Lord—the
temple, of course—is located on His mountain, Zion. The
nations wish to go to God's mountain to visit the temple. The
variation in divine names is interesting. "Yahweh" in colon A is
God's personal, covenant name, and "God of Jacob" identifies
God as the one whom the patriarch worshiped. It is unwise to
read too much into the variation. Certainly, in this case, the
variation is partly for reasons of aesthetics. "God of Jacob" is a
much longer phrase than "Yahweh," and so the prophet reaches
for near-equal length of lines by supplying the long name for
God in the second colon, which is missing the compound verb.

The next line is composed of two short cola that are nearly
equal in length:

> He will teach us his ways;
> we will go in his paths.

The two clauses have a similar word order that binds them
together. It is not obvious in the English translation, but both
cola begin with a verb and then end with a prepositional phrase
(the first colon is *midd^erākāw,* literally, "from his ways"). The
other binding feature is the nearly synonymous meaning of
"ways" (or "roads") and "paths." The second colon, though,
obviously advances the thought of the first and is not simply
saying the same thing twice. The relationship is one that often
occurs in parallelism. Specifically, the second line shows the
result of the action expressed in the first line. "He will teach us
his ways" *with the result that* "we will go in his paths." Of
course, "ways" and "paths" are a common metaphor in the Old
Testament for guidance.

The next line contains two cola that are nearly synonymous. I have preserved the word order of the Hebrew and have shown the grammatical functions in order to expose the chiastic binding within the line.

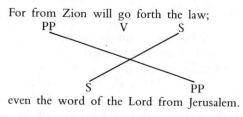

For from Zion will go forth the law;

PP   V   S

S   PP

even the word of the Lord from Jerusalem.

A chiasm is a crossing structure that may occur within a poetic line (occasionally also in prose), between two poetic lines, and even in much more elaborate structures. This line opens in colon A and closes in B with a prepositional phrase ("from"), and in the middle of the line the subjects appear ("the law" and "the word of the Lord"). This example is not simple chiasm because the verb that is elided in the second clause occurs in the middle of the first. While nearly synonymous, the second colon expands the thought of the first. "The law" (*tôrâh*) likely refers here to the first five books of Moses, while "the word of the Lord" may have a broader reference, perhaps including the prophets. Zion, of course, is the mountain of the Lord, located in Jerusalem. Jerusalem, the parallel to Zion, is the broader geographical area.

The next line is the longest one in the oracle, and the second colon is uncharacteristically longer than the first:

> He will judge between many peoples;
> he will settle quarrels for strong nations far away.

There is a clear parallelism here with the two verbs and the two prepositional phrases near in meaning to each other. The second line is longer because of the addition of modifiers. These modifiers (*ʿaṣumîm*, "strong"; *ʿad-rāḥôq*, "far away") provide more information to the thought of the first colon and in this way make the second colon more specific.

One of the most famous lines in Micah occurs next:

> They will beat their swords into plowshares;
> their spears into pruning hooks.

Once again the verb is elided in this verse. The two objects are both weapons, and the two prepositional phrases both mention agricultural implements. The mention of two weapons rather than one strengthens the impression that *all* weapons of war will be transformed into tools for the cultivation of the land, changing from tools of destruction into tools for cultivation.

The next line is not as clearly parallel as the immediately preceding examples:

> Nation will not lift up sword against nation;
> they will not even teach war.

Though there is not the kind of one-to-one relationship between words in this line, cola A and B are clearly related, and we may observe the typical intensification of thought that takes place between the cola. Not only will nations avoid active warfare (colon A); they will not even prepare for it (colon B).

The next line continues the theme of peace:

> A man will sit under his vine,
> and under his fig tree without fear.

The image evoked here is that of a man resting under a tree. It is a picture of peace and prosperity (see 1 Kings 4:25). The second colon both repeats the thought of the first and makes explicit that this resting is done devoid of fear.

A causal clause follows, and it is emphasized by being a monocolon in the middle of a number of bicola: "for the Lord of Hosts has spoken."

The concluding and climactic line is what has been traditionally described as an antithetical parallelism, a line that has two cola with contrasting perspective on the same idea:

> For all the nations will walk in the name of their god;
> we will walk in the name of the Lord our God forever
> and ever.

LUKE 1:46–55: THE MAGNIFICAT

The New Testament contains comparatively little poetry.[8] No single book is totally or even primarily poetic. We encounter only occasional, brief pieces of verse. Though rare, New Testament poetry is usually quite significant in its content. For example, the opening of the Gospel of Luke presents us with three important poems, the Magnificat of Mary (Luke 1:46–55), the Benedictus of Zechariah (vv. 68–79), and the Nunc Dimittis of Simeon (2:29–32). Paul occasionally interrupts the flow of his letters with an appropriate poetic hymn of praise (Phil. 2:6–11; Col. 1:15–20), and the Book of Revelation records poetic prayers and praise (e.g., 15:3–4).[9]

I analyze here the Magnificat.[10] Mary is visiting Elizabeth, the mother-to-be of John the Baptist, and in response to Elizabeth's greeting, Mary breaks out in a hymn of praise that bears close similarity to many hymns in the Old Testament, particularly to Hannah's song in 1 Samuel 2:1–10. The Magnificat is similar to Old Testament poems in both content and form. For instance, it displays the same type of parallelism that we have observed in various Old Testament passages.

The opening line is an unmistakable bicolon:

> My soul praises the Lord
> my spirit exults in God, my Savior.

Here both syntax and semantics are parallel. In terms of grammar, both lines begin with a verb, continue with the subject (both followed by the first-person possessive), and then conclude with a direct object (colon A) or a prepositional phrase (colon B). Furthermore, the second line affirms and progresses beyond the thought of the first. It frequently has been noted

---

[8] I thank my student Andrew Hwang for providing me with insights and bibliography on New Testament poetry in conjunction with a paper that he wrote on Philippians 2:6–11.

[9] See S. M. Baugh, "The Poetic Form of Col. 1:15–20," *WTJ* 47 (1985): 227–44.

[10] For previous analyses, see C. Tannehill, "The Magnificat as Poem," *JBL* 93 (1974): 263–75; and K. Bailey, "The Song of Mary," *Near East School of Theology Theological Review* 2 (1979): 29–35.

that it is out of keeping with the conventions of parallelism to contrast "soul" and "spirit" as two separate entities within a person. On the other hand, B does not just repeat A. Leon Morris has indicated that "exult" in the second colon is a much more intense word than "praise"; in the Greek, the verbs also differ in tense.[11] Furthermore, Mary's expansion of "Lord" into "God, my Savior" both identifies one specific function of the Lord and also personalizes the reference.

The parallelism loosens in the immediately following lines. A rough connection may be posited between the next three clauses by virtue of their each being a causal clause. Like all hymns the Magnificat provides reasons for the praise offered to the Lord. In the Psalms such reasons are normally introduced by the causal "for" (*kî*). In these three clauses the English "for" translates *hoti* (first and third clauses) and *gar* (second clause).

> For he has been mindful of the humble state of his servant,
> for from now on all generations will call me blessed,
> for the Mighty One has done great things for me.

The next two lines also are loose in their parallelism. Each meditates on a different attribute of God:

His name is holy
His mercy extends to those who fear him from generation to generation.

The next few lines delight in various actions that God has performed. The first colon gives a general description of those actions, followed by two that speak of His casting down the proud and the powerful. The third colon is antithetically parallel with the fourth, which contrasts God's humbling of the powerful with His exalting of the weak.

> He has performed mighty deeds with his arm;
> he has scattered those who are proud in their inmost thoughts.

---

[11] L. Morris, *The Gospel According to St. Luke* (Tyndale Commentary 3; Grand Rapids: Eerdmans, 1974), p. 76. The difference in verbs may reflect the common deviation between perfect and imperfect (*qtl/yqtl*) in Semitic poetry; see R. Buth, "Hebrew Poetic Tenses and the Magnificat," *JSNT* 21 (1984): 67–83.

> He has brought down rulers from their thrones,
>   but has lifted the humble.

The next bicolon continues the thought of the last two cola and is in a chiastic relationship with them:

> He has filled the hungry with good things
>   but has sent the rich away empty.

The last action of God is stated in verses 54–55:

He has helped his servant Israel, remembering to be
    merciful,
  just as he said to our fathers,
  to Abraham and to his descendants forever.

The last two cola are obvious related to one another by ellipsis and by the fact that the second line specifies the thought of the first.

EPILOGUE

The literary approach is, as we have seen, not really a method alongside of other methods such as genre analysis or editorial analysis. Moreover, it is certainly not a paradigm shift, as some have claimed. Rather it is one perspective among many by which an interpreter views a text. Because the literary approach is one perspective among others, we must resist the suggestion by contemporary literary theory that we deny or downplay historical reference of the biblical text in the face of its literary artifice. The Bible as literature *or* history is a false dichotomy. It is both and much more.

The literary approach, however, highlights an extremely important function of biblical revelation. As we have had occasion to observe many times, the Bible is more like literature than nonliterature. For the most part, we encounter stories and poems in the Bible, not systematic theology, pure historical report, or journalism. Why does the Bible have this form? Why did not God reveal to us His mighty acts in history in the form of a *Cambridge Ancient History*? Or why is the Bible not in the form of a systematic theology?

The ultimate answer to such questions rests in God's wisdom. We can discern, however, two positive functions of the literary form of the Bible. The first falls under the rubric of defamiliarization or distanciation. These two labels identify a concept discussed by Russian formalists, who describe the function of art as "the renewal of perception, the seeing of the world suddenly in a new light, in a new and unforeseen way."[1] To cast truth in the form of a story leads the hearer or reader to pay closer attention to it, to be shocked to reconsider what

---

[1] Jameson, *The Prison-House of Language,* p. 52.

otherwise might easily become a truism. A proverb is a good, focused example. Which communicates more powerfully, the simple imperative "speak righteously" or "the mouth of the righteous brings forth wisdom, but a perverse tongue will be cut out" (Prov. 10:31)? Which speaks more vividly, the bare command "love your neighbor as yourself!" or the story of the Good Samaritan (Luke 10:25–35)?

Second, literature appeals to the whole person. By its very nature, literature appeals not only to the intellect but also to one's will and emotions to a greater extent than, say, the Westminster Confession of Faith or Charles Hodge's *Systematic Theology*. We know and experience the power of stories and poems as children. Many, if not most, adults take less time to listen to well-told stories and striking poems.

We have recognized a tendency among some scholars to reduce the Bible to literature and to deny history. Other scholars, particularly those of us whose doctrine of Scripture is conservative, must resist the temptation to ignore the literary aspect of divine revelation by reducing the Scripture to history and theology. I have intended in this book to stimulate all of us to a more balanced reading of the Bible.

FOR FURTHER READING

A complete list of works cited may be found in the index of authors and titles. In this section I have selected contributions in English that should prove especially helpful as introductions to the major topics covered in this book.

A classic introduction to literary criticism is R. Wellek and A. Warren, *Theory of Literature,* 3d ed. (New York: Harcourt Brace Jovanovich, 1977). Balanced approaches to the study of prose literature may be found in W. Booth, *The Rhetoric of Fiction* (Chicago: University of Chicago Press, 1961); S. Chatman, *Story and Discourse* (Ithaca: Cornell University Press, 1978); and S. Rimmon-Kenan, *Narrative Fiction* (London: Methuen, 1983). A topically oriented handbook to literary criticism is M. H. Abrams, *A Glossary of Literary Terms,* 4th ed. (New York: Holt, Rinehart and Winston, 1981).

F. Lentricchia, *After the New Criticism* (London: Methuen, 1980) provides the best critical history of recent literary theory. For an excellent treatment of structuralism, consult J. Culler, *Structuralist Poetics* (Ithaca: Cornell University, 1975). For deconstruction, see J. Culler, *On Deconstruction: Theory and Criticism After Structuralism* (London: Routledge & Kegan Paul, 1982); and C. Norris, *Deconstruction: Theory and Practice* (London: Methuen, 1982).

Recently, literary critics have turned their attention to the Bible. The most notable example is R. Alter in his two books *The Art of Biblical Narrative* (New York: Basic Books, 1981) and *The Art of Biblical Poetry* (New York: Basic Books, 1985). M. Sternberg is an Israeli literary critic who has recently concentrated his skills on the Hebrew Bible. His book *The Poetics of Biblical Narrative* (Bloomington: Indiana University Press, 1985) is well worth reading, though it is verbose. F. Kermode deals with New Testament narrative in *The Genesis of Secrecy* (Cambridge, Mass.: Harvard University Press, 1979). Mention should also be made of two literary critics who hold to a conservative view of the Bible: C. S. Lewis, *Reflections on the Psalms* (Glasgow: Collins, 1961), and L. Ryken, *How to Read the Bible as Literature* (Grand Rapids: Zondervan, 1984) and *Windows to the World* (Grand Rapids: Zondervan, 1985).

153

Occasionally, biblical scholars analyze the use of literary theory in biblical studies. The most informative and well written is J. Barton, *Reading the Old Testament* (Philadelphia: Westminster, 1984).

Biblical scholars have produced a number of stimulating and well-written studies of particular sections of the Bible. It is in these studies that we find the best argument in favor of the literary approach to the Bible. Nonetheless, the reader must beware of the implicit or, occasionally, explicit denial of the historical function of the text. Good examples of the analysis of biblical prose include A. Berlin, *Poetics and Interpretation of Biblical Narrative* (Sheffield: Almond, 1983); C. Conroy, *Absalom Absalom! Narrative and Language in II Sam 13–20* (Rome: Biblical Institute Press, 1978); R. A. Culpepper, *Anatomy of the Fourth Gospel* (Philadelphia: Fortress, 1983); D. Gunn, *The Story of King David: Genre and Interpretation* (*JSOT* Supp. 6; Sheffield: JSOT, 1978); idem., *The Fate of King Saul: An Interpretation of a Biblical Story* (*JSOT* Supp. 14; Sheffield: JSOT, 1980); and D. Rhoads and D. Michie, *Mark as Story: The Introduction to the Narrative as Gospel* (Philadelphia: Fortress, 1982).

Biblical scholars have made dramatic progress in reading biblical poetry within the last decade. The single most important book is J. Kugel, *The Idea of Biblical Poetry* (New Haven: Yale University Press, 1981). Alter's book on poetry mentioned above follows in Kugel's footsteps and provides some illuminating readings of particular biblical poems. A. Berlin, *The Dynamics of Biblical Parallelism* (Bloomington: Indiana University Press, 1985) is for those interested in the grammatical aspects of parallelism. W. G. E. Watson, *Classical Hebrew Poetry* (*JSOT* Supp. 26; Sheffield: JSOT, 1984) is a comprehensive handbook of biblical poetics.

INDEX OF BIBLICAL PASSAGES

INDEX OF MODERN AUTHORS
AND TITLES

INDEX OF SUBJECTS

(All dates are A.D. unless otherwise noted.)